THE
MIRACLE
OF
MILK

PORTRAIT OF THE AUTHOR

The Miracle *of* MILK

How to Use the Milk Diet Scientifically at Home

BY

BERNARR MACFADDEN

AUTHOR OF "MACFADDEN'S ENCYCLOPEDIA OF PHYSICAL CULTURE," "EATING FOR HEALTH AND STRENGTH," "STRENGTHENING THE EYES," "HAIR CULTURE," "MANHOOD AND MARRIAGE" AND OTHER WORKS ON HEALTH AND SEX.

APPLEWOOD BOOKS

The Miracle of Milk was originally published in 1924 by
Macfadden Publications, Inc. of New York City.

Thank you for purchasing an Applewood Book.
Applewood reprints America's lively classics—
books from the past that are still of interest to
modern readers.

ISBN 978-1-55709-511-4

Library of Congress Card Number: 00-110662

PREFACE

MILK is the greatest of all diet cures.

It is already scientifically combined.

When you are furnished with this delectable fluid you need not bother about other nourishment.

"Milk for babies, water for weaklings and women, and whisky for men," is an old time quotation, but it is out of date.

This age would doubtless interpret it, "Whisky for fools, water for men, milk for babies and invalids."

And that is our position. An invalid is a weakling. In functional strength he is a mere baby, and that is why milk is so valuable under such circumstances.

I have personally come in contact with thousands of people who have been amazingly benefited by adhering to the exclusive milk diet.

I have personally secured benefits at different times in my own life that could not be measured in money value.

John D. Rockefeller, the richest man in the world, advertised nearly thirty years ago and offered a million dollars for a new stomach. I never heard of any one accepting this offer, but a short time after that reports were frequently circulated of his interest in outdoor life, golf, etc., and now, at his greatly advanced age, it is reported that he lives exclusively on milk; that he is maintaining his life at his present great age because of this simple diet.

The milk diet, properly prepared for and properly used, is capable of bringing about miraculous changes in the physical organism. We are presenting, in the following pages, the amazing truth in reference to this remarkable diet.

There are times in the life of every human unit when the milk diet can be of extraordinary value. Whether you need it now or in the future, it will be of inestimable value to you to assimilate carefully the information contained in this book.

It will undoubtedly give you more life while you live and it may add many years to your life. It may actually save your life in a crisis when a simple, invaluable food can be used advantageously.

The facts presented in this volume are of but little value if hurriedly scanned, but if read and absorbed they will offer you an equipment of knowledge that will be invaluable.

In the writing of this book I have not only gleaned from every phase of my own experience, but I have been aided by an editorial staff who searched in every possible source for additional information on this important subject. Medical and literary experts have materially added to its scope.

More than twenty years have elapsed since I first tested the value of this diet in a régime, and the longer I live, the more I study it, the more I am able to appreciate it.

I am quite sure that the experience of the readers will be similar, if they give the subject proper attention.

Bernarr Macfadden

CONTENTS

IMPORTANT
NOTE

THE reader should not attempt the use of the Milk Diet until he has thoroughly familiarized himself with its procedure by the careful study of the instructions of a book such as this. For the reader's convenience in reference, a Summary of the Milk Diet briefly explaining each step of the treatment is given at the close of this book (pages 198 to 204). While this Summary will be helpful to the reader in crystallizing his understanding of the principles of the treatment and at the same time serve as a guide during the practice of the régime, it will still be necessary for him to study the text of the book before he may safely undertake the treatment. Benefit can be derived only by the correct practice of the Milk Diet, and such correct practice is impossible without a full comprehension of principles, which is to be reached only by attentive reading.

The Miracle of Milk

CHAPTER I

Why the Milk Diet Cures

EARLY HISTORY OF MILK AS FOOD.—MILK THE ONLY
PERFECT FOOD.—NEED FOR MORE MILK.—HOW
MILK CURES.—COMPOSITION OF MILK.—ITS MIN-
ERAL SALTS.—NOT DEFICIENT IN IRON.—FINEST
FAT IN THE WORLD.—CALORY VALUE OF MILK.—
CONTAINS ALL THE PRINCIPLE VITAMINES.—ITS
ACID-NEUTRALIZING VALUE.—ITS LARGE WATER
CONTENT.—REDUCES TOXINS.—EFFECT ON BLOOD
AND LYMPH AND THEIR CIRCULATION.—BUILDS
RICH BLOOD. — INCREASES LEUCOCYTES—WHITE
BLOOD CELLS.—REACTION OF SKIN AND NAILS TO
THE MILK DIET.—SKIN ELIMINATION INCREASES.—
FLUSHES IMPURITIES FROM THE SYSTEM.—GREAT
VALUE AND IMPORTANCE OF MILK IN CHILDHOOD.
—MILK BOTH A FOOD AND MEDICINE.

FROM the earliest dawn of human history milk has been recognized as one of
the most valuable of food products. In fact,
the cow, next to the dog, was probably the
earliest domesticated of the animals. For,

away back in pre-glacial days—before the great ice-flow changed the surface aspects and the climate of Europe—the Swiss Lake-Dwellers kept cattle, the milk of which, reinforced by the fish they hauled out of the lake, furnished their chief source of food.

Wells tells us that it was in the Neolithic Age, ten or twelve thousand years ago, that the nomadic hunter evolved into the herdsman, and mankind first became cow-keepers. The practice of cow-keeping gradually spread all over the earth, until now there are very few races, civilized or savage, city dwellers or nomads, in Europe, Asia or Africa, who have not depended, or do not depend, more or less, upon cow, goat, reindeer, or buffalo. And, as we all know, among many African tribes the wealth of an individual is measured by the number of cows he owns. Indeed, a man may even buy his wife from her loving father for a certain number of cows, depending upon the youth and comeliness of the maiden and upon how badly he might be smitten by her charms.

Millions of people, as the Tartar tribes

in Asia and many of the Central European races, even now find in milk and in milk products their principal source of nutriment.

And so free from disease are they that certain of these peoples, such as the Bulgarians, have been given credit for being among the longest-lived of all the peoples of the earth. In fact, Metchnikoff's famous discovery that age-decay is largely the result of the absorption into the system of poisons generated by decomposition in the intestinal canal was stimulated by the study of the diet of these same Bulgarian peasants, who lived largely upon clabbered milk—milk fermented by adding a little of the clabber of the preceding lot. This "cultures" the milk, causing the development of large quantities of health-giving lactic acid germs.

These germs are supposed to destroy the colon bacilli and other more highly toxic bacteria that breed in the intestinal canal, and thereby prevent their destructive action upon the delicate nerve cells and upon the general organism.

In our own country an average of between

half a pint and a third of a quart of milk is consumed every day in the year by every man, woman and child in the land. This amounts to from twenty-five to thirty million quarts of milk each day for the country as a whole. Probably as much again goes to the manufacture of butter, cheese, and other milk products.

On the Continent, two or three times as much milk and products derived from milk are consumed as are consumed in the United States, but regardless of the considerable amount of milk that is used daily, comparatively few people here or elsewhere are using milk as an exclusive article of diet for the treatment of abnormal conditions, either functional or organic. The milk industry is of vast importance to the country and community because of the exceptionally valuable nutritive qualities of milk and our absolute dependence upon it as an indispensable food for infants, young children and invalids, and because of the actual therapeutic or curative properties of milk when properly used.

4

THE FOOD VALUE OF MILK

Indeed, the food value of milk can hardly be overestimated. This may be better visualized by remembering that a quart of milk equals in food value three-quarters of a pound of beefsteak, two pints of oysters, eight eggs, two pounds of chicken, three-fifths of a pound of pork chops, or three pounds of fresh codfish.

When one is securing, then, from four to six quarts of milk daily (the usual amount taken on the full milk diet) one can see that the body is securing a large amount of most valuable and wholesome nourishment. Owing to the selective action of the cells of the body and because every necessary element is furnished to normalize functional processes and make it unnecessary and practically impossible for the cells to take up an excess of a certain element, all of any particular element that is supplied above the absolute demands of the human economy for wear and tear, maintaining and increasing weight, and repair work is expelled from the body through normal eliminative channels.

This is decidedly opposite to the action of the system when given the usual conventional diet. In such a diet the system is not supplied with every requisite element, but receives some far in excess, with few corrective, normalizing elements. The final result is an exhaustion of certain functions and a deposition of toxic elements in certain tissues.

When we grasp the significance of these facts we can readily understand that it is more milk, rather than more meat, that the people need, and insofar as the production of meat interferes with the production of milk a great evil arises. Milk is an invaluable food, and every means, not excluding the total elimination of meat as food, should be adopted to increase its use. I have no doubt that our devotion to the fleshpots is the greatest single factor in the present restricted use of milk, which is the most unfortunate phase of our dietetic habits. In fact we could well dispense with the packers altogether, if such a consummation would result

6

in an increased supply and a proper consumption of this most valuable food substance.

To answer to the question, "How does milk cure?" we need to know only that it furnishes elements necessary to make new blood. Milk is one of the most easily digested and assimilated foods, containing ample amounts of substances required for the growth of tissues and organs and the repair of worn-out cells.

When one is taking the milk diet he does not have to worry about combinations or whether this element or that element is being supplied. Every element is there in the milk in living organic form, and the sick body uses them to the best of its ability—and·it is well to say that that ability is constantly increasing as the milk diet is followed day after day and week after week.

Milk is the best food in that most precarious period of life—babyhood; and it is also the best food in that other critical period, whether of the babe or adult—chronic illness. Some have said, "Milk is food for babies, not for adults." This is true, and that is just why we prescribe it for sick people. No sick person is an adult. Let him first restore his enervated, functionless, depleted, emaciated, worn-out old body to normal functioning and normal proportions before he claims maturity, and this is done in the large majority of cases more surely, safely and satisfactorily by taking the milk diet than by any other known method.

WHAT MILK IS

Milk is a watery solution of albumin, milk sugar, and certain salts, holding fat globules in suspension. The protein and the mineral matter are in semi-solution. When taken from the cow milk has a slight alkaline reaction, but this changes rapidly to a very slight acid, due to the rapid development of lactic acid bacilli.

Whole milk should have a specific gravity of from 1.029 to 1.035, pure water being reckoned at 1.000. It should contain not less than 8.5 per cent of solids, apart from fat—and not less than 3.25 per cent of butter-fat.

According to Dr. Henry C. Sherman, professor of Food Chemistry at Columbia University, milk consists of proteins 3.3 per cent, fats 4 per cent, milk sugar 4.8 per cent, citric acid, 0.1 per cent, ash constituents 0.7 per cent, and water 87.1 per cent. The albumin and casein of milk rank at the head of the list among proteins.

No sugar, with the single exception of dextrose (the finished product of carbohydrate digestion), is so easily assimilated as lactose, or milk sugar.

Among the mineral salts of milk we find sulphur, phosphorus, chlorine, sodium, potassium, calcium, magnesium, iron and iodine— all indispensable elements in supplying nutritive material for the brain and nerve cells and essential for building strong bones and perfect teeth.

The iron of milk is very small in amount (only 0.00024 per cent). Yet it is rapidly absorbed and completely utilized. So that, notwithstanding the small amount of iron taken into the system with milk, the improvement in the iron content of the blood is often more marked and much more rapid than while taking meat and other iron-forming foods.

Time and again an increase of from fifty to seventy per cent in the hemoglobin of the blood in anemic individuals has been observed.

In fact, on the basis of from twelve to fifteen milligrams of iron per day being required to replace the "iron loss" of the system, and on the basis that there are .24 milligrams of iron in each 100 grams of milk, five or six quarts of milk per day will supply the amount of iron needed each day by the human system.

BUTTER FAT

When a drop of milk is put under the microscope, the fat globules are readily seen floating in the serum, or fluid portion of the milk.   These fat globules are among the most finely subdivided or emulsified of all the fat globules to be found in Nature. A drop of milk the size of a pin head may contain 1,500,000 of these tiny droplets—which explains why the fat globule of milk is perhaps the most easily digested and assimilated of all fats.

There is no finer, richer fat in all the world than the butter fat suspended in infinitesimally small globules in the milk. But never, or at least rarely, will the full fat content of milk be digested and absorbed. The unnatural products resulting from the changes in the fat may produce disturbance throughout the digestive tract, and may result in sufficient irritation to produce a diarrhea or nausea and vomiting. For these reasons it is quite frequently necessary to reduce the amount of cream considerably.

Of course, the great bulk of the milk is water—to be exact, about eighty-seven per cent. Yet, when considered from the standpoint of its health value, this wealth of water is a distinct asset, especially among a people who rarely drink as much water as they should, and who, as a consequence, suffer

from constipation and imperfect elimination
of effete body material.

Indeed, were plenty of water to be taken
at all times, it would normally be excreted
through the kidneys and through the bowels.
The feces would be softened and rendered
much more voidable by the solvent and stimulating action of the water. The considerable amount of water secured on the full
milk diet is of distinct value in helping absorb and eliminate toxins and acids from the
system.

THE CALORY VALUE OF MILK

The calory, or heat and energy producing
effect of milk, varies according to the amount
of fat contained in the milk.

Average milk, with four per cent of butter
fat, yields about 675 calories per quart, at
314 calories to the pound. Skim milk, while
equally good as a tissue builder, quite as rich
as is whole milk in vital mineral salts, and
equally satisfactory as a healing diet, contains much less of calory value, as only from
eighteen to twenty per cent of the calories

are furnished by the protein of the skim milk, the remainder by the milk sugar.

However, it must be remembered that the calory is, after all, only a unit of measurement—nothing that contributes to the nutritive value of the food it measures.

THE VITAMINE CONTENT OF MILK

Within the past few years marvelous discoveries connected with the health-giving aspects of milk have been made by Hess, McCollum, and other scientists, as well as by the Children's Bureau of the United States Public Health Service.

Briefly, these authorities have found that many diseases, some of them so grave as to cause even death, as well as serious physical and mental deficiencies, may arise as a result of the lack of protective foods—foods rich in mineral salts and in the vitamines.

"It is recognized," says U. S. Public Health Service Bulletin No. 325, "that although vitamines undoubtedly are widely distributed in food products, they occur for the most part in very minute amounts, and the various foods differ in the proportions which they contain. If the diet is made up principally of foods poor in vitamines, or rendered so by their preparation, an insufficient amount of these substances would be provided, and abnormal metabolic processes would result."

In this connection it is interesting to note that milk· has been found to be among the richest in vitamines of all foods. While there is, as yet, no exact means of measuring actual amount of vitamine substance, it is definitely decided by repeated experiment that milk contains large amounts of the Vitamine A, as it is called. This is the vitamine upon which growth largely depends, and which has so frequently been found missing or deficient in the case of rickity, marasmic babies, stunted children, and backward adults.

The "nerve-feeding" Vitamine B, the lack of which causes paralysis, beri-beri, and various other grave nervous disorders, is also found to be abundant in whole milk.

The anti-scorbutic factor, the principle

14

that prevents scurvy, is also abundantly present in milk.

It is evident from this that if one were taking the milk diet these grave disorders would never develop. Since the elements are present in milk which would prevent the development of such disorders, they are present in such form and in such amounts as to cure conditions when they develop, if the strict milk diet is taken.

Milk contains also several important ferments which aid digestion, such as diastase, galactose, etc. These ferments or digestants undoubtedly act as stimulators and regulators of nutrition, and are identical in their function with certain of the digestive enzymes secreted by various organs in the body.

Because of its mineral salt content, milk, especially an exclusive milk diet, markedly increases the alkalinity of the blood. Remember that the normal alkaline state is the state of highest health and physiological functioning, while the acid state is the pathological condition.

The contributing cause of many of the

most serious of all disorders—such as diabetes, Bright's disease,. rheumatism, high blood tension, etc.—is an over-acid state of the system. This condition is rapidly overcome by the alkaline salts of milk, which explains why the exclusive milk diet, or the milk and fruit diet, is so generally effective in these conditions.

Because of the large amount of fluid absorbed when on the absolute milk diet, toxic elements in the tissues are highly diluted. And because of the natural tendency of the blood to maintain a certain degree of concentration, it has a very much more pronounced tendency to absorb deposits in various tissues and structures when on the milk diet.

THE EFFECT UPON BLOOD AND CIRCULATION

One of the most outstanding effects of the full milk diet is the marvelous effect the ingestion of this large amount of fluid has upon the circulation. This is most important, from the standpoint of normal functioning. For many people suffering from chronic diseases are troubled with defective circulation of the blood. Their blood pressure is thirty or forty degrees below or above what it should be. This condition may manifest itself by cold feet, cold hands, constant chilliness, susceptibility to colds, and numerous other symptoms.

These are the cases that respond very rapidly to the effects of the full milk diet. This is due to the improved circulation and to the increased amount of life-giving fluid in the veins and capillaries. Often within a few hours after commencing the diet their pulse rate will be increased when very low. Inside of forty-eight hours the heart beat has frequently gained four or five beats to the minute. The pulse will be full and vigorous and the blood will flow to every cell and tissue in the body with increased force.

The dry, scaly character of the skin will disappear and instead there will be a healthy moistness and glow in its surfaces. The colorless, leathery skin covered with pimples and eruptions becomes rosy and clear, and free from unsightly blemishes.

The prolonged baths taken as part of the treatment, as will be described later, assist in softening up the harsh outer layers of dead skin and facilitating their removal. Perspiration is increased and the pores of the skin are stimulated to throw off dead material that might otherwise accumulate in the deeper tissues of the skin and in the deeper, more vital organs of the body.

Not infrequently when patients first begin the milk diet they will awaken from sleep completely bathed in perspiration—sometimes of a most offensive character. This is not due to any weakness or to a thinning of the blood, as some patients fear, and as occurs in the night sweats of the consumptive, but is due to increased activity of the circulation and increased power of the sweat glands to rid the system of poisonous materials. Often the sweat will be found to have a very unpleasant odor, and that of rheumatic patients will not infrequently have a strong odor of urea.

The large accumulations of waste materials when the skin is frictioned, as in massage, prove conclusively the health-giving benefit of this treatment. Even the nails share with the skin in the obvious benefits of the milk diet—their rigid roughness giving way to a smooth, normal condition, showing the improvement in the purity of the blood and the increased alkalinity of the body fluids. All this, remember, while the patient may be perfectly quiet in his room or even while lying in bed, such is the deep effect of a full milk diet.

The benefits of this improvement in the circulation must be conceded by every medical man, for there is nothing in their entire armamentarium of drugs, exercise, massage, baths, oxygen inhalation, electric treatment, or blood transfusion can equal the natural physiological increase in blood circulation that is brought about as a result of increasing the amount of circulatory fluid in the veins and arteries of these debilitated patients.

TOOTH AND BONE NUTRITION

The lime, phosphates, fluorin, and other mineral salts in milk also have a very definite

19

constructive value in building tooth and bone cells, as these salts are found in rich profusion in milk and in the most easily assimilable form.

Milk contains practically twenty different chemical elements, which makes it of enormous value as a general building food.

And this applies not alone to bone and tooth structure, but also to brain and nerve cells—which can not function without lime and phosphorus—and to various of the ductless glands, which depend upon lime, phosphates, and sodium salts to stimulate their normal functioning.

MILK—THE PERFECT BUILDING DIET

Also, milk contains leucocyte cells, not unlike the white blood corpuscles of our own blood. There can be little doubt but that these are absorbed into the circulation, to reinforce the white cells already in the blood stream in overcoming disease germs that may have gained entrance through the respiratory passages, or been absorbed from the stomach or bowels into the blood stream.

20

WHY THE MILK DIET CURES

After the first feeding of milk these cells have been known to increase from five to six times their usual number in a given amount of blood.

Since the various mineral elements, tissue-building elements, and leucocytes are absorbed in considerable numbers, it is easy to account for the rapid subsiding of inflammation, and for the rapid repairing of wounds and injuries, when the full milk diet is supplied.

There is no doubt but that the nutrient material in the milk can be absorbed directly into the lacteal vessels of the intestines, from which it can be taken up at once by the blood.

It is a fact that milk is secreted directly from the blood, and that its serum, or fluid portion, is practically identical with blood serum.

The fat droplets of the milk, it is certain, can be absorbed and utilized at once to become a part of the fatty portion of the blood.

The milk sugar (the carbohydrate portion of the milk) can be absorbed and assimilated without undergoing any further process of

21

digestion (after coagulation)—some maintaining that milk can be completely absorbed from the colon, when given as a nutrient enema. Also, there is a small proportion of fibrin, or coagulating element in milk, identical with that found in the blood. This partially explains why one is less liable to severe hemorrhages after a regular, systematic milk diet.

Therefore, it is obvious that no other dietary article so adequately fills the growth and health requirements of the body as does milk, and that no other dietetic régime can compare in simplicity and yet in effectiveness with the full milk diet.

It is highly probable that if the five million American boys and girls whom the Federal Department of Labor reports as suffering from malnutrition in its various forms could only have the proper amount of milk, *given in the proper way,* their malnutritive condition would be a thing of the past, and abounding health and vitality would replace their present lamentable health deficiency.

In fact, so convinced am I of the value of

milk, both as a food and as a medicine, that I am willing to go on record as stating my belief that, without a doubt, ninety per cent of all the malnutrition among children everywhere could be cured if two quarts of milk a day were supplied to each child. I heartily agree with Dr. Graham Lusk when he states that no family of five can afford to purchase a pound of meat until it has first bought at least three quarts of milk.

This is a lesson every man, woman and child in this country should take to heart. It would mean an increase of millions of work-hours, and a longer, healthier and happier life for everybody, if they did.

But when these physical abnormalities have developed or begun to develop, in adult or child, feel assured that the diet that would have been effective in preventing illness and in maintaining health will be effective as a curative agent when taken correctly, after proper preparation, and with the proper adjuncts, as will be described in a later chapter.

CHAPTER II

When to Use the Milk Diet

FUNCTION OF FOOD.—MILK FULFILLS ALL SPECIFICA-
TIONS.—MILK WILL SUSTAIN HEALTH AND LIFE
INDEFINITELY.—USES OF MILK AS A MEDICINE.—
DOCTORS' OPINIONS.—THE MILK DIET IN HEALTH.
DISEASES CURED BY A MILK DIET.—ITS ALMOST
UNIVERSAL APPLICATION.—MILK DIET REMOVES
UNDERLYING CAUSES OF DISEASE.—BENEFITS OF
MILK IN ABNORMAL BLOOD PRESSURE.—HOW THE
MILK DIET AFFECTS DROPSY.—EFFECT ON WEIGHT.
—MILK AS A CURE FOR DIABETES.—WHEN THE
DIET MAY NOT BE ADVISED.—RUPTURE AND THE
MILK DIET.—MILK IN MODERATION IN EPILEPSY.
—DR. RICHARD CABOT ON TAKING MILK.—INDI-
VIDUAL ADJUSTMENT NECESSARY.

THE function of food is to nourish. Food
is any substance which, when taken into
the body, will supply nourishment to tissue,
repair damaged tissue, and supply heat and
energy, without producing any deleterious
effects. Any substance which fails in any
one or more of these specifications, is not a
food and should not enter the body. That

food is best that provides the maximum amount of nourishment with the least expenditure of digestive energy, and that creates the smallest amount of organic debris, and of the least harmful nature to be eliminated.

This must not be taken as an endorsement of the so-called "concentrated diet" — the minimum requirements of our dietary put up in tablet or capsule form—as tried out by the German chemists some years ago.

For we know that a certain amount of "bulk" or "roughage" is indispensable. This gives the bowel muscles substance upon which they may act, and material with which the highly toxic broken-down cell tissue can combine, the more readily to be eliminated. However, a happy medium is to be found in the exclusive milk diet, or in a combination of milk with the pulp and juice of a few oranges (from one to three) per day.

Upon this diet one can live indefinitely, maintaining at the same time the very maximum in physical and mental efficiency. When the diet and the mode of living in other respects have been such as to produce disease, (unless a disease is acute and associated with fever, when fasting is the only proper dietetic measure to adopt) then the milk diet is, by far, the most satisfactory diet to restore health, in practically every instance.

The use of milk as a distinct curative agent dates from the very remotest period. Hippocrates, the Father of Medicine, advised consumptives to drink freely of asses' milk. Whey, the watery portion of sour milk, was recommended highly by the Arabian physicians, who were, by all odds, the most successful and the most scientific of all the medical practitioners of the Middle Ages.

The credit for popularizing the use of milk as a medicine, however, must be largely ascribed to Russian and German physicians. Many German dietitians were enthusiastic advocates of the "milk cure." One of the most famous of these, Prof. Bauer, says:

"It is an indisputable fact that in certain diseases a methodical use of milk gives results such as can be accomplished by no other form of treatment."

Dr. Inozemtseff, as far back as 1857, published a work on "The Milk Cure" in which he detailed successful results on upward of a thousand cases.

Dr. Philip C. Karell, in August 1866, published reports showing the successful use of milk in hundreds of cases of dropsy, neuralgia, rheumatism, asthma, disorders of the liver, and many forms of mal-metabolism. He called attention to the fact that milk and chyle (the milky fluid found in the lacteal glands after the ingestion of food) had a great resemblance to one another.

Many American and English physicians have called attention to the almost specific value of milk in acute Bright's disease. Dr. Johnson, a famous English physician, states that "in numerous cases of acute Bright's disease, the speedy disappearance of the albuminuria under the influence of rest in bed, a few warm baths, and copious libations of milk was nothing short of marvelous."

This same treatment was equally successful in several bad cases of inflamed bladder. Weir Mitchell, who was recognized as one of the staunchest believers in the milk cure in America, and who had an enormous experience in treating disease with rest and the milk diet, once said: "it is difficult to treat any of these cases without a resort at some time more or less to the use of milk."

Dr. L. Duncan Bulkley, head of the New York Skin and Cancer Hospital, contends that milk can be absorbed from the lacteal glands directly into the blood.

It seems strange, in a way, that anything so simple and so lacking in mystery as milk should effect cures with such uniformity, and in grave disorders that have resisted the efforts of the most skilful medical men, armed with the most heterogeneous assortment of drugs and poisons, and that it should be prescribed or even appreciated by so few physicians as it is.

Yet, such is the case. By a means so simple that even a school boy could carry it out, thousands of people all over the country are now curing themselves of grave ailments

—particularly of the chronic type—many of which have been pronounced incurable by eminent physicians.

The exclusive milk diet should not be prescribed, ordinarily, for one who is in good health. It is an upbuilding diet for those who have been suffering with disease and are struggling to get back to normal health as speedily and perfectly as possible.

In all cases of acute disease, especially where there is fever, the milk diet or any other diet should not be prescribed, except in some few instances where it is given in very small quantities to excite the digestive function of the stomach and intestines. Fasting, or near fasting, is the proper practice in such cases. This holds true even in tuberculosis, unless the victim is already greatly emaciated and exhausted.

The effects that are desired in treating fever can be far more readily and speedily obtained, without the slightest danger, by withholding all foods except water.

THE MIRACLE OF MILK

The milk diet is very broad in its application. There are few exceptions to its general helpfulness. These exceptions will be taken up later in this lesson.

There is hardly a disease of metabolic origin—which includes every possible disorder of digestion, assimilation and elimination—which can not be materially helped and often completely cured by a properly taken "milk treatment."

Also, many diseases supposed to be of germ origin, which can be self-limited through increasing the defensive powers of the body, are curable by this treatment. Among the many disorders successfully treated are nervous troubles of all sorts—including insomnia, neuralgia, neuritis, headache and migraine, nervous prostration and nerve irritability; also general debility, and stomach and intestinal indigestion, and their resulting auto-intoxication; ulcer of the stomach and intestines, acid stomach, and dilation of the stomach; prolapse of the

30

stomach, intestines, kidneys, or uterus; pimples, boils, carbuncles, sallow, blotchy complexion, eczema, dandruff, anemia, biliousness, catarrh of the air passages or of the digestive tract, constipation, chronic diarrhea, and dysentery, asthma, hay fever, hardening of the arteries, piles, chronic appendicitis, rheumatism, arthritis and lumbago, hives, ovarian trouble and leucorrhea, impotence, liver trouble and gallstones, Bright's disease and diabetes, tuberculosis in the early stages, and narcotic habits of all kinds. Also, in abnormal blood pressure conditions, whether too low or too high, the milk diet works almost miraculously.

By this it will be seen that the milk diet is usually successful in apparently very widely differing conditions; but practically all disease is the result of a disturbed balance of the circulation, with congestion in some parts and anemia in others; or a deficiency of elimination with retention of waste materials in the body which produce disease in some organ by lowering its vitality, or which produce symptoms in some other part of the body as the system endeavors to eliminate them; or to exhaustion of certain organs and functions through over-stimulation and constant enervation as the result of endeavoring to keep the body purified and free from encumbrance.

Even the so-called contagious and infectious diseases would not be possible if one's blood stream were absolutely free from excessive nourishment and toxins, and if it contained every health-maintaining element. But as few are in this condition, these diseases develop. And because of wrong—suppressive—treatment at the time, and also because of the marked reaction of the body tissues and chemicals to the disease and drugs, certain organs and fluids and body chemicals are thrown out of balance and remain so in many instances long after the "disease" itself has subsided.

All of these conditions lower the vitality and it is in such a physical condition that many symptoms and so-called "diseases" develop.

It should, therefore, be clear that a full,

nourishing diet, that is easy of digestion and that contains no toxin-producing residue, is essential in the restoration of health. Such a diet is the milk diet as herein considered.

Malnutrition may be the result of any one or more of several conditions—inherited weakness, vaccination, suppression of acute disease by drugs, or coddling in childhood, or a grossly wrong diet leading to constipation and disturbance of the vital forces of the body. Also to destructive habits which throw the chemical nature of the body out of normal equilibrium, or which directly injure nerves or tissues.

Since in all of these conditions it is essential to eliminate drug poisons and the body poisons they were given to suppress; and since it is necessary to equalize the circulation, to nourish the nerves and tissues and restore them to normal functioning ability, to rid the tissues and the blood of toxins and acids of a destructive nature, and to restore normal equilibrium in the chemistry of the body, it is absolutely necessary to supply a food which will accomplish this without, in any degree, tending to defeat its own purpose. Such a diet, without doubt, is the milk diet; and, except in a few instances, there is no other diet that will approach it in effectiveness. These other instances are not in the field of dietetics, but in individual cases of disease.

MILK DIET IN ABNORMAL BLOOD PRESSURE CONDITIONS

Patients suffering from anemia, auto-intoxication, and many wasting disorders, who are almost invariably below normal in blood pressure, are benefited to an extraordinary degree.

And, as previously stated, if the blood pressure is abnormally high, or the heart-beat abnormally fast, the milk diet will lower the pressure and decrease the rapidity of the heart-beat.

Those who have arteriosclerosis, or hardened arteries, bronchitis, asthma, or kidney disease, are generally benefited by the exclusive milk diet, their blood pressure often being reduced ten to thirty degrees within a month—probably to the neighborhood of one hundred and thirty degrees, which is about normal for the average adult.

So, when the blood pressure is too high, or too low, the tendency is for it to come down or come up to normal, during or by the expiration of a course of the full milk diet adjusted in amount, method of taking, and time, to the individual case.

Usually in the beginning of high blood pressure there is no organic change. Through over-activity of certain glands of the body during an attempt to combat excessive toxins, or from constipation, heavy diet of wrong foods and wrong combinations, and many other conditions that should be temporary if properly adjusted, the blood is sent through the blood vessels at greater force and at greater speed. This physiologically increases blood pressure, but such a blood pressure will vary, with success or defeat of the body in removing its toxins. But in course of time if the causes are allowed to continue, Nature, ever on the lookout for self-preservation, produces a change that eventually defeats her aim. She causes a thickening of the walls of the blood vessels, possibly with deposits of earthy mineral elements, to combat the increased pressure. This produces such an organic change that the blood pressure is consequently more or less permanently high.

As the milk diet is free from an excess of mineral elements, and as it supplies a large amount of fluid which makes it necessary for the blood to absorb from tissues certain extraneous elements in order that it may maintain approximately its normal degree of saturation, this diet, when taken exclusively, has a marked tendency to reduce blood pressure even after an organic change of hardened arteries, or arteriosclerosis, has been established.

In a low blood pressure there is usually, as indicated above, anemia or wasting disorders. As the milk diet normalizes the blood, thus making it possible to feed every tissue and structure of the body, including the blood vessels, and as it gives sufficient quantity of blood for the heart to pump through these blood vessels, the blood pressure is restored quite rapidly to normal, with a resulting improvement of the general condition.

With these cases rest in bed or at least much rest and relaxation during the treatment is important—in fact, really necessary.

HOW THE MILK TREATMENT AFFECTS DROPSY

People who suffer from dropsy need not hesitate for a moment in adopting the milk treatment. For, notwithstanding the apparent absurdity of adding three or four quarts of fluid to a system that seems to be already suffering from a superabundance of it, the dropsical condition quite uniformly yields.

The quantity of urine voided immensely exceeds the quantity of milk ingested, proving that the milk definitely excites a freer elimination from the kidneys as it does from the skin and bowels.

Dropsy is usually associated with heart or kidney disease, or local obstruction to the circulation. In a case of heart disease the milk aids in reducing the inflammation or abnormality of the heart itself, or at least it

37

greatly reduces the toxic elements in the blood which aggravate the existing organic lesion. It also relaxes the capillaries of the skin, which not only reduces the work required by the heart in pumping the blood through these capillaries, but also increases skin elimination: this helps the excess of fluid to escape through the skin. Not only this, but the large amount of fluid of the milk which enters the blood reduces kidney congestion because of the diluted urine; and the large quantities of urine passed will contain much of the edematous fluid, as the diluted blood will take up some of this fluid, which is heavier than the blood of the milk diet patient, in order to maintain its normal degree of saturation.

If the dropsy is due to kidney disease, the remaining active tissues of the kidneys are able to pass off larger quantities of fluid because they are handling a more diluted fluid. In addition, the circulation is greatly improved and this aids in carrying fluid to the kidneys, and the kidney inflammation is allowed to subside because of the bland fluid passing through the kidneys. In this case also the skin activity is increased and this eliminative organ carries off larger quantities of fluid.

HOW MILK DRINKING AFFECTS WEIGHT

It has been observed that, practically without exception, a rapid increase in weight follows the taking of a full milk diet by those who are below their normal weight. This result is practically uniform. Thin, emaciated people frequently take on weight extremely rapidly; for their tissues are invariably undernourished, and respond rapidly to the nutrient effects of this most easily assimilated of all diets.

Those who are merely thin, and who are not the victims of some grave, wasting disease, may expect to gain anywhere from one to seven pounds a week. A gain of from one to three pounds a week may persist for several months—until they are once more up to their normal weight.

The gain from this milk treatment is good, healthy tissue—not soft, flabby fat, as so frequently follows the use of some of the so-called fattening foods, which are largely carbohydrate and do not contribute to actual nutrition, except by furnishing heat and energy to run the body machine.

Nor need fear be felt that any gain made on milk could have a harmful effect. For tissue built up out of milk can not form fat, to clog and hamper the vitally important work of the heart and the internal organs.

The muscle cells themselves will actually increase in size under a milk diet, because they become filled with rich blood. Therefore, the cheeks plump out, the flaccid breasts become more firm and shapely, the limbs take on a more symmetrical appearance — the entire aspect changes for the better.

And when to this is added a buoyancy of spirits, a clearness of eye, an alertness and a vivid interest in the things that make life worth while, it can be understood that, from a standpoint of mere beauty and charm, the milk treatment is in a class by itself.

But not only is the milk diet effective in

increasing weight. It has been used with success in cases of obesity, where it is desired to lose many pounds. In real obesity the fat is thin, flabby, and watery. The milk has the same effect here that it has in cases of edema. Besides, when on the proper milk diet there is a great reduction in the amount of fattening foods consumed, as fat people are almost universally heavy consumers of foods rich in fattening elements. Also, there is frequently a lack of chemical balance which is corrected by the milk diet. But ordinarily these cases can not consume the large amount of milk taken by emaciated individuals, as their digestion and assimilation (particularly the latter) are extra good. It requires less food taken into the body to supply the same amount of nutriment—it requires less to maintain wear and tear.

No definite amount of milk can be stated here as that required to allow one to lose weight, but an excellent feature of the diet is that the quantity is so easily adjusted to the needs of the body that one can easily determine for himself the amount required to lose from one to three pounds a week. I might say that the average amount would be from two and one-half to four quarts a day.

DIABETES AND THE MILK DIET

A Dr. Donkin first employed the milk diet treatment for diabetes, fifty-five years ago. These patients were given as much as fourteen pints of milk daily.

No diabetic should attempt the milk treatment until he has fasted a few days in order to make the system more sugar-free, and to give the assimilative organs a better chance to "take hold" of the milk.

Some diabetics have complained that the sugar output was increased on the milk diet, and that the acetone and diacetic acid was also increased in amount.

This is sometimes the case when whole sweet milk is used. For sweet milk contains five per cent of lactose, or milk sugar, and about four per cent of butter fat. This high sugar content would overload the system with an unoxidizable amount of sugar, and will sometimes greatly aggravate the gen-

eral diabetic symptoms. The very heavy fat
content would stimulate the production of
acetone, and in some cases might possibly
bring about the dreaded diabetic coma.

It is for these reasons that we usually give
skimmed sweet milk in cases of diabetes. In
some instances the milk need not be fully
skimmed, but usually it is best to use milk
without cream, at least for the first two
weeks of the milk treatment. I also advocate the use of buttermilk, or a low-fat
sumik (to be described in Chapter III) in
these cases. For, in the process of developing the lactic acid of the buttermilk, and in
the souring of milk for sumik, a large per
cent of the sugar content of the sweet milk
is transformed. Also with skim milk soured,
or a low-fat sumik, only a minimum of fat
is introduced into the system to prove a men-
ace in the formation of acetone.

DISEASES IN WHICH MILK IS
CONTRA-INDICATED

There are but few diseases in which the
use of milk would be absolutely contra-in-

dicated. Chief among these are "contracted kidney," where the most important eliminating organ is badly damaged by atrophy of its cells.

In case of rupture, as the milk diet has a tendency to enlarge the abdomen temporarily and to increase the intra-abdominal pressure, this diet is not of particular benefit; and if the rupture is of considerable size, the milk as a sole article of diet is contraindicated.

However, I believe that if one wears a well fitting truss, takes the corrective exercises on an inclined table, uses the cold applications or cold sitz baths, possibly and for the most part takes the milk in bed, the milk diet, slightly limited in quantity, may be taken for some other condition where it is indicated without disturbing the rupture.

As epileptic attacks are frequently brought on by a full stomach, the milk diet is usually unsatisfactory in these cases. But even in this condition, where a fast has preceded the diet, and where a quantity of no more than three or four quarts of milk was taken daily, and where care was observed to keep the bowels free from accumulated debris, considerable benefit has been secured in many cases.

The milk diet has a tendency to fill and probably distend the bladder. In certain cases of prostatic enlargements a full bladder makes it impossible or very difficult to void the urine. In these cases the milk diet is not satisfactory unless taken in small quantities, as in epilepsy.

Some claim that in arterial degeneration, and where apoplexy is to be feared, also in aneurism, it would be well to avoid the increased tension that may be brought about by milk. But my experience is that these cases require the beneficial effects of the milk diet, and that it can be safely given in a limited quantity *after a necessary fast.* These cases, however, *must* take the rest cure during the milk treatment, for safety and for best results.

For patients who have been recently operated upon, or who may have a ruptured blood vessel, it is best also to prescribe a fruit fast and then the limited milk, taken while resting. For that matter, practically every case, regardless of the nature of the disorder, should begin treatment with a fast. The main difference in the above case is in the quantity of milk given and the necessary rest —in bed constantly except for the period of the bath.

In experience with thousands of cases I am convinced that the milk diet properly adjusted to the individual case is of tremendous value in practically any functional or organic disturbance that may affect the human body.

I agree with Dr. Richard Cabot who says: "Any one can take milk. If a person tells me, 'I can not take milk,' I always say, 'you can, if you will take it a certain way'." But the diet must be adjusted to suit the individual condition and requirements. When this is done, one may benefit by the marvelous effects of the milk diet.

CHAPTER III

The Milk Diet Régime—How to Use It at Home

MILK DIET MUST BE TAKEN PROPERLY.—HOW TO
PREPARE FOR THE DIET.—WHAT KIND OF MILK
IS BEST.—SKIMMED MILK.—BUTTERMILK AND
SUMIK.—CANNED MILKS.—HOW TO START TREAT-
MENT.—PRELIMINARY FAST.—THE MILK DIET
SHOULD BE EXCLUSIVE.—DAILY QUANTITY OF
MILK.—WATER DRINKING WITH MILK.—DURA-
TION OF TREATMENT.—MILK AND LABOR.—BEST
TIME FOR TREATMENT.—FRESH AIR.—EXERCISE.
—MENTAL ATTITUDE.—DAILY WARM BATHS.—
TOBACCO A DETRIMENT.—READING MAY INTER-
FERE.—SEXUAL INDULGENCE DURING TREATMENT.
—EMERGENCY ALTERNATIVE RÉGIMES.

THE average individual who has given
little or no thought to the subject of diet
in general and less to that of milk, is inclined to make two errors in regard to this
diet unless especially cautioned.

He is apt to begin the milk diet directly
on discontinuing solid food without any
preparation of the digestive tract, and be-

cause milk is a liquid he is inclined to drink
it as water is taken. Another mistake that
might be mentioned is that of imagining one
is on the milk diet when perhaps two or three
pints are taken daily—in cases where several
quarts are required; or when two or three
meals of solid food are taken, and milk used
in quantities of several pints between meals.
The mere mention of these ideas as mistakes
is sufficient to indicate that they should be
avoided.

While I do not believe in the taking of
medicine in liquid, powder, tablet, or other
form, yet because of its healing and curative
effects, milk may be rightly termed a medicine—one of the most valuable, yet least
generally appreciated medicines that we
have. And to secure the most satisfactory
results, preparation must be made to take
this "medicine diet," and it must be taken
with considerable regularity, as other medicine is prescribed.

Many times I have found that individuals
have been impetuous and eager to get on
to the milk diet, under the wrong impression

that the milk was the only curative part of the dietetic régime—that the fast was merely to allow the stomach to empty itself and secure a short period of rest. While the milk is curative, the preliminary fast may be even more so, especially in many toxic and infective conditions.

In many other instances, this same impetuosity leads one to consume from twenty to fifty per cent more milk than is required —either by drinking more at a time, shortening the periods between "doses," or lengthening the number of drinking hours. Unless one is extremely careful to take proper preparatory treatment, to begin the milk treatment properly, and to conduct this treatment properly throughout the course, the results are not apt to be to his entire satisfaction.

HOW TO PREPARE FOR THE MILK TREATMENT

In preparing to take the milk treatment, it would be well to provide for the maximum degree of rest and relaxation. Though it is possible to take the treatment successfully while still pursuing one's daily tasks, the results are usually not so good as they are when the cure is made the principal object of interest, and not merely an incident.

Further, the responsibilities of business and the time required for its conduct prevent that regularity in taking the milk which is one of the most important features of the treatment.

Therefore, as much as possible, all organs, except of course the digestive and the eliminative organs, should be afforded as complete a rest as possible.

Provision must be made for frequent opportunities to urinate. For naturally when five, six or more quarts of fluid are drunk every day, the kidneys must operate actively in order to carry off the extra fluid and the waste that is brought away with it.

If it is decided to take the treatment practically in bed—as may be necessary in treating Bright's disease, well advanced diabetes, tuberculosis, or many prostrating or crippling disorders—great care should be taken to insure the maximum degree of comfort by selecting the proper kind of bed and the proper kind of mattress.

The bed should be preferably of iron, as an iron bed is usually more sanitary and is less liable to the creaking and squeaking associated with a wooden bed—sounds which often distract the sleep and render it less restful and health-building.

The bed covering should be light but warm. Sleep between sheets, but see to it that, if weather conditions require extra covering, plenty of light woolen blankets cover the sheets, so that the skin may breathe and the perspiration may be absorbed.

This will necessitate frequent changes of bed-clothing, and more frequent airings, in order to keep the bed clean and sweet. But it is very essential that the skin, which is one of the most important of all organs of elimination, be given the fullest chance to function properly.

There should be one gown for night and one for day. These should be soaked in some cleansing or disinfecting solution, and rinsed out after each using.

WHAT KIND OF MILK IS BEST

My own experience inclines me to believe that, whenever it is possible to secure it, the best milk, either for the "milk cure" or for general uses, is good, clean milk, unaltered in any way since coming from the cow— free from the addition of any preservative substances, and untampered with in any respect.

I realize that, unless one lives in the country, contiguous to the source of supply, it is difficult to secure milk of this character.

There is, in larger and smaller dairies alike, the very general, though not universal use of chemical preservatives. This is to prevent the development of acid-forming bacteria, and to prevent abnormal fermentation of the milk.

The manufacturers who sell these products and many of the dairymen who use them may conscientiously believe them to be harmless, even for long continued use. I do not share in this belief.

Some of these mixtures with a borax

"base" may not be exactly poisonous. But they certainly render the milk much less digestible. Therefore, in an invalid or in a weak baby, they might actually constitute themselves a predisposing cause of some grave digestive disturbance, or even of death itself.

Others among these preservatives, such as formaldehyde, formalin or salicylic acid, are distinctly poisonous. Many States recognize this fact and forbid their use and sale.

There is, in my judgment, no harmless preservative for milk; for whatever will prevent fermentation will render the milk less digestible, and therefore less valuable as a food.

There has also been a great deal of discussion as to what kind of milk is best to use. As one individual cow's milk is very likely to vary from day to day, it is always preferable to use milk from a herd or dairy rather than that from a single cow. I am convinced that Holstein milk is best; then that from Ayrshire, Shorthorn and Durham cows, and last of all milk from pure bred

Jersey and Guernsey, or Alderney cows. If, however, milk from Jersey cows is to be used, it should invariably be partly skimmed, after standing two or three hours, in order that the cream content may be reduced.

It is well known that the Holstein, Shorthorn, and Durham cows are rugged and not subject to diseases, especially tuberculosis, as are Jersey cows. And it has also been occasionally observed that Jersey cows sometimes give milk that the young calves can not digest. This is because of the considerable amount of cream and the large size of the fat globules — two conditions that tend to render milk indigestible.

We frequently give skimmed milk and with better results in many instances than could be secured from whole milk. For skimmed milk has all the nourishing elements of whole milk except that perhaps half the fuel for heat has been removed in the cream. The milk sugar and protein, however, will supply all the heat necessary.

Many people who take up the milk diet for the purpose of putting on weight make the great mistake of attempting to use an eccessive amount of cream.

Cream does not tend to increase flesh in the body, although it does conserve or prevent the breaking down of fleshy tissue, or protoplasm, by being more readily available as immediate fuel.

The tissue built up when taking milk is formed almost entirely from the albumin, casein, and lactose or milk sugar. Too much cream or fat in combination with this casein would actually defeat the purpose for which the cream and rich whole milk was intended to be taken.

GOAT'S MILK

Emphasis has probably not been placed by those recommending the milk diet upon the value of goat's milk. In many sections of the country it is impossible to secure this milk, since goats are not kept; but in some districts large herds of goats are kept for milking purposes. In these localities one may take goat's milk for the milk diet.

Those who find cow's milk disagreeing for

any reason may find goat's milk satisfactory in every way. The fat globules of the latter are much smaller than in cow's milk. even in Holstein milk, which condition has a tendency to reduce fat indigestion. The cream rises less rapidly, maintaining a more perfect emulsion for a longer time.

The ruggedness of goats makes them less susceptible to disease, and their milk may, therefore, be less contaminated. It has a slightly different taste, but the majority of individuals find it as agreeable as that of cow's milk.

BUTTERMILK AND SUMIK

Buttermilk is also of value in some cases. Lactic acid fermentation has soured the milk, thus completing a part of the digestion outside the stomach. As most of the fat is removed on churning, the digestion of this food is further hastened. The difficulty is that one is apt to tire of the taste of this milk much sooner when on the full milk diet than on sweet milk or sumik.

Wherever buttermilk is of value, and this

is usually where acid is lacking in the stomach, sumik may be used. This is a clabbered milk made as follows: Set away unpasteurized milk (or pasteurized milk if *only* this can be obtained) in quart bottles or other air-tight containers, in a warm place for twenty-four to thirty-six hours or until clabbered. If the sumik is not to be used immediately, put it on ice until needed. If kept in a warm place it will become too sour and the curd and whey will separate, which condition makes the milk less desirable. Just before using beat well with a rotary egg beater.

Sumik may be taken as an exclusive diet, or, if there is no particular digestive disorder, a few dates or some other sweet fruit may be taken with it. If, for any reason, sweet milk can not be taken, buttermilk or sumik should be given a trial.

I remember one young man who had abhorred milk from childhood who could take sumik with relish, from which he derived the same benefits as from fresh milk. However, he finally developed a liking for fresh milk.

As a matter of convenience, and where it
is impossible to secure supplies of fresh milk,
it will be found that dried or dehydrated,
powdered milk, or condensed or evaporated
milk offers a fairly effective substitute.

These milks, of course, contain most of the
mineral salts and protein found in the whole
milk. Certain brands of the dried milk, however, are deficient in fats, which would seem
to be an asset, instead of a liability.

It is also a fact borne out by many hundreds of feeding experiments that, in a number of cases, dried milk is markedly more
digestible than ordinary milk.

One of the most certain ways of determining the efficacy of any form of milk is in its
effect on the growth and nutrition of infants,
who, of course, are peculiarly susceptible, as
they get practically no other food from which
they can secure missing food elements, as do
adults.

One of the best tests of rickets or malnutrition is to check up in the infant the time at which independent walking commences. This is ordinarily found to be within fourteen months. If the ability to walk is delayed materially beyond this period, it is generally indicative of malnutrition.

So it is interesting to note that children fed on dried milk and the proper fruit acids walk almost as early as when they have been fed on a whole milk diet, and have apparently quite as good a resistance to disease, and are practically as well nourished as are children who are fed on whole cow's milk. So, as regards dehydrated milks producing scurvy, there need not be the slightest apprehension—if fruit acids are taken. Without the latter, I believe the results could not be as satisfactory as with whole fresh cow's or goat's milk.

Certain vitamine tests, made recently, seem to indicate that the fat-soluble A Vitamine, in particular, is very resistant to heat. Osborn and Mendel, and also McCollum and others, have shown that this vitamine found in butter fat will resist the temperature of live steam without destruction. Dry heating at a temperature of 212 degrees Fahrenheit, with free access of air, only very slowly destroyed the fat soluble vitamine. Water-soluble B (antineuritic vitamine) also resists high temperatures to a considerable degree.

While it therefore appears that the heat used in pasteurizing, boiling, evaporating, condensing, and drying milk has apparently very little effect upon these two vitamines, such milks do not contain the life force and the mineral elements in such sufficient quantities that they can replace fresh milk completely. They are not entirely satisfactory for a perfect milk diet régime, such as is discussed in this volume. But that they are valuable sources of nourishment in certain conditions and circumstances can not be denied, and they are worth trying if raw milk can not be secured.

HOW TO START TREATMENT

In order to obtain the best results from the milk treatment it is advisable (unless the individual should be unduly weak and debilitated) to give the system a thorough chance to rest and make ready to absorb the health-giving milk. For when the organs of digestion and elimination first have a chance to rest and fit themselves for their task, the improvement and assimilation are much more rapid.

This complete rest can best be secured by a fast of a day or two. If you are plethoric and overweight, with a sluggish condition of the glandular system, it might be well to extend the fast to as long as five days, or even a week.

It is rarely advisable to prolong the fast much beyond this period, unless under a physician's care, nor is it usually necessary. For by this time the system will usually have unloaded itself of much of its accumulated poison, and the stomach and the system generally will be in a good condition to benefit by the treatment. But if a fast is progressing favorably, no time limit should be set for it.

It is sometimes advisable to eat acid fruit,

instead of fasting completely, as the acid
fruit tends to stimulate the activity of the
liver and bowels, besides building up the alkaline reserve of the blood by means of its
alkaline bases. This is particularly true of
the citrus fruits — oranges, lemons, and
grapefruit.

THE MILK DIET SHOULD BE EXCLUSIVE

It must be distinctly understood that with
the exceptions mentioned here and to be further mentioned in Chapter IV, no other food
than milk is to be taken while you are on the
"diet." I mention this for the reason that
many have told me they have taken the milk
diet without results, and upon inquiry I
usually find they have taken three regular
meals with whatever milk they were able to
drink at and between meals, and have im-
agined they were on the milk diet. Such a
procedure is not "dieting" but "stuffing."

Unpasteurized milk should be secured *if
possible*. If not, by taking orange, lemon
or grapefruit juice along with it, pasteurized
milk may be used.

The milk usually should be cool. Where there is poor circulation and slow digestion, or during cold weather, the milk should be warmed to body temperature. It should never be boiled and, in fact, never heated over one hundred and ten degrees.

Some practitioners claim that the milk is best tolerated when taken at "room temperature," not lower than sixty-five degrees. Others find that if milk is warmed to body temperature it is more readily digested.

This is largely a matter of individual preference, and must be gauged by personal experience. If it is deemed best to warm the milk, this can most readily be done by putting the glass of milk in a pan of hot water, leaving it until it is of the desired temperature.

A pan of water may be kept on the back of the stove or radiator for this purpose, or it may be found desirable to use an electric plate under the pan. Under no circumstances use a vacuum or thermos bottle, as the milk may tend to spoil in sustained artificial heat that is not sufficiently hot to sterilize. And never put a pan of milk directly over the fire unless it is extremely carefully watched to prevent scorching. If this method is employed the milk should be stirred constantly.

HOW MUCH MILK SHOULD BE TAKEN

The amount of milk to be taken depends entirely upon the condition of the patient, the condition of digestion, and whether one has been fasting a few days or many days, or eating regular meals previously. After a fast, it is necessary to begin milk gradually, the amount and rate depending upon the length of the fast. After a two or three day fast, take a glass of milk every hour on the first day, and every half hour thereafter for a period of twelve hours daily. After a fast of four or five days or longer, take a glass of milk every two hours on the first day, every hour on the second, and every half hour thereafter, for twelve hours daily. This last method may also be employed in most cases after fasts as long as ten days to two weeks, though it may be necessary to take smaller amounts for the first day and then follow with this plan.

Most adult male patients who have taken the milk treatment have found that the average amount they can take with comfort is eight ounces, or a glassful, every half hour—after this amount has been reached by the above plan. Women usually find four and a half to five quarts a day sufficient—approximately one quart a day less than men. They sip this slowly, or take it through a straw, to facilitate the mixture of the milk with the saliva. Often they chew gum for five minutes, following each glassful. This they sometimes find to be of considerable benefit in aiding digestion. The gum used should be paraffin or other totally unflavored gum. But avoid this whenever possible.

The stomach after a fast is contracted, and the musculature, not having been exercised as usual, is weak; therefore its work must be taken up gradually, just as we begin exercise gradually after a rest cure. On the other hand, if the milk is taken immediately following a regular diet, a glass should be taken every half hour from the very first day. Some prescribe a glass every half hour while the patient is awake, but in a twelve-hour period enough milk is taken, and the twelve hours' rest is beneficial. Those following this plan are stronger after completing the diet, and retain the weight gained.

The ideal amount is between five and six quarts daily. This is as much as anyone can successfully digest. Observe that I say *successfully digest*. It is true that many can push seven, eight, and even ten quarts of milk through the alimentary tract, but this milk is not digested, as has been proved many times by chemical examination of the feces. Positively less milk may be digested and assimilated on a large quantity than on a smaller quantity, because of the energy depression and energy dissipation through *trying* to digest and eliminate the excess over requirements.

The safe rule may be given as that which allows as much milk as can be *comfortably digested,* up to six or seven quarts a day as the usual maximum. But the stomach should be kept working close to its capacity during the milk drinking hours, when on this diet. Pay no attention to appetite and hunger. If no milk is taken during the night (and except in rare instances this should be the rule), there is usually a morning hunger that lingers for the most of the succeeding day, and the milk is relished. It is the amount of milk *digested and assimilated* that is curative, and not that which is passed through the body. One man took but three quarts per day and gained five pounds in a month. Many others have done almost equally well. Still, in a few unusual cases three times this amount has been taken, relished, and apparently normally digested.

Perhaps as satisfactory a plan as any for arriving at the most suitable quantity of milk is to take a quart of milk for each twenty-five to thirty-five pounds of body weight. As we can not give a definite amount that will be perfectly agreeable in every case, this plan usually can be followed safely. Much depends upon the type of individual, and upon how nearly any particular case conforms to the average normal for that type.

A man six feet tall may weigh one hundred and thirty-five pounds and another of equal height may weigh two hundred and fifty, and neither one appear to be particularly seriously handicapped. But as the thin man should weigh more, he will require considerable milk to supply his defective digestive and assimilative organs with sufficient nourishment on which to gain; whereas the heavier man, whose digestion and assimilation are good, will require less to produce desired results, while still allowing him to reduce to a more nearly normal weight.

While a man weighing normally (not from fat) two hundred pounds will naturally require considerably more milk than one weighing normally (not emaciated) one hundred pounds, he will not require *twice* as much. For the former, six to seven quarts daily will be a low enough maximum—and it is occasionally safe to allow a two hundred pound man of the "raw-bone," or all bone and muscle and no fat type, as much as eight quarts a day; while for the normal hundred pound man five quarts would be a liberal maximum, and four, or four and a half quarts at the most, would usually be safer. The normal man of five feet eight inches will weigh one hundred and fifty pounds. Six quarts daily will be his usual maximum quantity, and many of these men will make more progress on from five to five and a half quarts. But the six quarts per day may be considered a good average from which to work in deciding the most beneficial quantity for other weights, following the plan of a quart for each twenty-five to thirty-five pounds of body weight above or below the normal 150 pounds.

A woman's frame is generally smaller, the texture of her tissues finer, her physical and physiological activities less pronounced. For these reasons, a woman will usually require daily, as I have stated elsewhere, about a quart of milk less than a man, even of the same height. The average normal woman is about five feet five inches in height and weighs about one hundred thirty-two pounds. She should use in ordinary cases about five

quarts daily. Larger and smaller women
can use this as a guide for securing the
amount most suited to them.

Another rough guide is to take one quart
of milk for each foot of height. This will
apply for men, while women should use
three or four ounces less per foot of height.

I might say here that one-eighth ounce
glass of milk every half hour, or a pint every
hour for twelve hours will give six quarts;
a glass every forty-five minutes, or a pint
every hour and a half for twelve and a half
hours will give four and a half quarts; and
a glass every hour for twelve hours will give
three quarts. By this one can easily keep
account of the amount consumed.

If one desires to take about five quarts of
milk daily (which is the average "full quantity" for women) a forty minute schedule
may be followed—continuing the milk from
say, 7:30 a.m. to 8 p.m. Or, the regular half
hour schedule may be used from 7:00 a.m.
to 7:00 p.m., and the milk omitted at four
periods during this drinking time; or by de-
laying the beginning in the morning, or dis-

continuing the milk sooner in the evening, or both, the same may be accomplished. Quantities other than the regular five quarts or six quarts (for women and men respectively) may be taken regularly by adjusting the schedule by scme such method as just given, but as nearly as possible keep the drinking hours down to twelve, that the stomach may have a considerable period of rest. If more than six quarts is to be taken daily, shorten the periods between glasses or, after the first few days, take a larger amount at each drinking period, rather than increase the length of the drinking hours.

I realize that one taking the milk diet has little time for other occupation—visiting, picture shows, etc.—but if the highest beneficial results are expected, nothing should be allowed to interfere with the régime. Some, however, do well by taking a pint every hour, which plan gives them more time between drinks for any necessary work, shopping, etc. But social obligations should never interfere with a health-restoration program.

71

The milk should be sipped slowly. It is very important that the milk enter the stomach in small amounts. The smaller the sips the smaller the curds in the stomach and the better the digestion. If taken as one drinks water, large, difficultly-digested masses are formed. The preferred and, in fact, the ideal way to take milk, and the manner that more nearly simulates the nursing baby's way, is to close the lips very tightly over the rim of the glass, the edges of the lips barely covering the rim of the glass, with a very small opening. This plan necessitates a vigorous sucking in order to draw the milk into the mouth and this sucking produces a contraction pressure upon the salivary glands, forcing their secretion into the mouth and in contact with the milk, to dilute it and to help produce smaller curds when the milk passes into the stomach. Besides, the milk tastes better when taken in this manner, and both salivary and gastric juices flow more freely. This naturally favors more nearly normal digestion of the milk.

THE MILK DIET RÉGIME

It must not be taken for granted that the milk diet is suitable for the correction of disorders in adults alone. Children and young people respond even more marvelously to the treatment than do their elders.

However, if children are properly treated in their acute disorders they will respond so thoroughly and satisfactorily that there will not be the innumerable symptoms and disorders prevalent in adulthood.

Of course, the proper procedure with children is so to order their diet and general mode of ilving that they will not be susceptible, even, to the acute disorders. But if these precautions to prevent or properly correct acute disorders and illnesses are not observed, and it is necessary to adopt some curative measure for some sub-acute or chronic disturbance, then the fast and milk diet régime is the most satisfactory that can be devised.

Not only in acute disorders should the fast

be given in childhood as well as in maturity, but it should precede the milk diet in cases of longer standing. Because of the usually greater ability to respond to favorable treatment possessed by children, a shorter fast will usually bring about satisfactory results. Two or three days of water only, or of water and fruit juices, or acid fruits alone, may be taken preparatory to the milk diet with safety.

The milk diet should be taken by children after a definite schedule the same as it should be by adults. The quantity necessary will vary with them, naturally, according to their age and size and general physical condition.

Youths and misses of sixteen to twenty can usually take as much as the adults of their sex. Boys of perhaps thirteen or fourteen to sixteen usually require about as much as an adult woman—four and a half to five quarts a day. Girls of this age will require a pint to a quart less.

Equal amounts will be required by children of both sexes at younger ages. Three to three and a half quarts of milk a day will probably be sufficient from eight or nine to twelve or thirteen years of age, depending upon the already mentioned conditions. Even younger children may require this amount, but children from five to eight will rarely require over two and a half or three quarts a day.

Children of a year or so will require three pints or somewhat more or less. And from this amount to two and a half or three quarts will be required from weaning time (one year or so) to four or five years of age.

The remainder of the treatment—that is, the application of the adjuncts mentioned in the next few pages—will be the same as in adults, though naturally adapted to the individual case and condition.

SHOULD WATER BE DRUNK?

The question is often asked as to whether or not it is desirable to drink water while taking the milk course. There can be only one answer to this: Let your appetite be your guide. If you crave water, by all means drink it. However, in consideration of the fact that milk contains about eighty-seven per cent of water and that you are getting anywhere from four to six quarts of fluid each day, it would hardly seem necessary to take into the system further quantities of a fluid deficient in food material.

In obesity, however, it would be well to take all the water you care for, reducing the quantity of milk accordingly. For the desideratum here is to take more fluid and less food, so as to stimulate a freer excretion of waste products, and thereby force the system to oxidize its excess of stored-up fat.

HOW LONG SHOULD THE MILK DIET BE CONTINUED?

It is natural to ask how long should the milk diet be continued. To this I would answer, the longer the better. That is, until all symptoms have disappeared—at least the most troublesome and significant symptoms, or, if for any reason this is impossible, then until they have been greatly relieved.

In some cases the treatment may have to be alternated with a fast several times, until the purpose is effected. In others, a period of meals may alternate with the diet. In such cases it is customary to take milk for from four to six weeks, followed by two weeks on the solid diet, after which the milk is resumed if necessary. One should remember that the body requires time to overcome the injuries of years of wrong living, and because health does not follow a few weeks of the milk diet it must not be considered a failure. It must be repeated over and over again until health is attained. *The principle of cure is correct,* and the results are uniform if the method is correctly followed.

One patient remained on the diet for eighteen months before he was able to digest solid food. His final improvement and gain were all he could have desired. In some cases a few weeks will suffice to restore a person to normal. A Dr. Taylor of Croydon, England, over two hundred years ago, cured himself of epilepsy in two years with the milk diet, and lived on milk exclusively for seventeen years thereafter.

This answers very effectively those who

maintain that man can not live on milk alone. I believe that man can live in better health and do more real work while living on milk than on any other diet whatsoever. We must first get the idea out of our heads that the body needs a large amount of solid nourishment, represented by a large number of calories or heat units.

Milk is so easily digested and assimilated that a much larger amount of real nourishment is obtained from it than from the large meals of solid food thought necessary for adequate nutrition. It is all very well to figure up the calory content of a meal, but who knows how much of the food is digested, assimilated, and used by the body?

LIVING ON MILK FOR FIFTY YEARS

In one case, quoted by a milk diet specialist, a patient has lived on a strictly milk diet for more than fifty years. He has never been ill a day in all that time, and his bowels have moved with absolute regularity twice a day.

This gentleman, as it happens, was forced

by necessity to go on a milk diet, for at the age of two he took a dose of concentrated lye. This caused a stricture of the oeso- phagus, or food pipe, which has prevented him from swallowing solid food of any kind. The passage was so constricted by the effect of the lye that not even a crumb of bread could pass through it.

Yet this man is rugged, healthy and well nourished, the father of four robust children. All the food he has ever had in these fifty years has been a quart of milk at each meal.

This proves that certain individuals have wonderful powers of assimilation, enabling them to utilize practically every grain of food value in their allotment of milk. Doubt- less the milk diet itself has a great deal to do with establishing a perfect assimilation and function. Were this not so, this man could hardly have secured from the relatively small amount he was taking the necessary material to meet all needs of cell growth and repair, and at the same time secure the req- uisite amount of heat and energy to give him the abounding vitality he is credited with possessing. But this experience is by no means unique.

Professor Weir Mitchell in "Fat and Blood," says: "I have seen several active men, even laboring men, live for long periods on milk, with no loss of weight; but (frequently) large quantities have to be used. . . . A gentleman, a diabetic, was under my observation for fifteen years, during the whole of which time he took no other food but milk, and carried on a large and prosperous business. Milk may, therefore, be safely asserted to be a sufficient food in itself, even for an adult, if only enough of it be taken."

However, we are dealing here with the milk diet as a therapeutic measure. In by far the majority of cases a milk diet for from four to six weeks, or a series of milk diets alternated with fasts for a period of two or three months, will suffice to normalize and regulate the organic system and numerous functions, so that it will not be necessary to continue for long periods of time on this diet. These cases are cited merely to prove that milk, even when taken exclusively, contains every element necessary for maintaining health. And what will maintain health will correct the large majority of disturbances of health. The effect of citing these instances may also encourage those who should continue a curative régime for a long period of time to do so. Also, if one prefers to continue on the milk diet for the purpose of developing the highest degree of health possible, he may be assured that it is perfectly safe in every way for him to continue this as long as desired or required. In fact, experience has shown that it is better to err on the side of continuance of this diet than in any way to curtail it.

One may do an immense amount of physical and mental labor and be extremely active during this diet. It has also been noted that such individuals are able to endure extremes of heat and cold better than the average person living on the ordinary diet. In fact, it has been claimed that one may get more out of a quart of milk than an Eskimo can extract out of a pound of blubber.

Probably the best time of the year for the milk diet is Spring and early Summer. At this time of the year the cows are eating new grass, which seems to give the milk a greater curative value, probably on account of the increase of the organic salts and the better health of the cattle when outdoors and eating their natural diet. This will apply mainly, however, to cows in large dairies.

The majority of people throughout the country will be able to secure milk from cows that are out of doors practically the year round. This tends to keep the cows in good health. Also many farmers have silage to feed their cattle during the winter months. So far as chemical analysis is concerned, there may not be a great deal of difference in milk secured at various seasons because of the fact that the cow's system and udder is a laboratory which tends to produce a certain quality of milk. If the food elements are absolutely lacking, this can not be done without producing disease in the cow through her system's effort to supply the elements to the milk by taking them from her own body tissue and fluid.

However, judging by many years' experience, with thousands of cases treated the year round, I believe that the milk diet can be taken at any time of the year with practically uniform benefits, with possibly a slight advantage of Spring and Summer milk over Fall and Winter milk. If you find that you require the milk diet, do not hesitate to take it because the season has passed for the cattle to receive fresh grass and green stuffs. Take it at whatever time of year you need it, regardless of season, and expect favorable results.

PLENTY OF FRESH AIR

Provision should be made for securing plenty of fresh air—day and night. Except in extremely cold weather, or during heavy storms, at least one window of your living and bed rooms should be opened wide. Or, better still, two windows, especially if situated on the same side of the house or in right-angle walls so as to avoid drafts over the bed, should be open, to favor a free circulation of air at all times.

Remember that food has to undergo a process of oxidation or combustion before it can be utilized to yield heat and energy, or before the "end products" of the albumin elements can be burned up into harmless "ash," to be excreted by the kidneys and bowels, skin and lungs.

Therefore deep breathing exercises are of great value, and all means should be utilized to provide the lungs and the blood with ample quantities of oxygen to carry on the vital processes of the body.

EXERCISE AND THE MILK DIET

There are two distinct thoughts in regard to exercise when taking the milk diet. Some claim that there should be a complete rest in bed in all cases. Others advocate exercise generally, and advise a complete rest in bed only in certain cases. Exercise will tend to aggravate the condition where there is complete exhaustion of vital forces; where there is neurasthenia to an extreme degree; whenever movement excites considerable pain, especially of an inflammatory nature; when the blood pressure is excessively high, or where apoplexy is imminent or has already visited the patient; where fever is present, as in tuberculosis and acute illnesses; in cases where diarrhea is pronouncedly aggravated on exertion; where the muscular or valvular condition of the heart is dangerously diseased; where there is considerable pathology in the kidneys, or infection elsewhere in the abdomen or pelvis; where there are stones in the kidneys, or bladder, or gall-bladder; and in prolapse of any abdominal or pelvic organs, if the exercise is taken in the upright position. But in practically every other instance exercise will be of advantage.

The greatest value of exercise when on the milk diet is in the fact that it increases the depth of respiration and the amount of fresh air taken into the lungs. In every instance, however, one should avoid such fatiguing excess of exercise as may cause debility or throw into the circulation a greater

amount of fatigue poisons (the by-products
of broken-down cells) than can be got rid of
by the oxidizing effects of deep breathing
and the recuperative effects of sleep.

If your condition necessitates a complete
"rest cure" in bed, it is advisable to take exercise only in the form of passive motion
or tensing of the various muscle groups while
lying in bed. The former is motion of the
joints given by an attendant. Also stretching of all the skeletal muscles in the body
will be a very great help.

Or a daily general massage, either by some
masseur or masseuse called in for the purpose or by some member of the family, will
stir the sluggish circulation and facilitate
the removal of waste products from the system, thereby hastening the progress of the
cure.

Owing to the fullness of the abdomen after
a few hours of the milk diet, it is usually
preferable to take the daily exercise the first
thing in the morning, before any milk has
been consumed. If fruit juice is taken before beginning the milk, it is usually better

to take the exercise even before the fruit juice, but after a glass of water. However, if it has been found that the fruit juice will not cause any disturbance when followed immediately by exercise, there should be no harm in making it a rule to take the fruit first.

Those who are taking the milk diet for general upbuilding, without any serious physical disorder, may take exercise an hour or so after discontinuing the milk at night, provided there is no distress during nor after the exercise and no diarrhea produced.

Sometimes a person has a "muscle hunger" which passive motion and stretching exercises do not fully relieve. In these cases, and in any other where it is apparently safe, one may take a short walk in the forenoon, or in the afternoon, or before retiring at night; or a walk at any two or all three of these times if strength and general condition permit—always starting out at least fifteen or twenty minutes after a glass of milk. This walk will assist in the peristaltic or churning action of the stomach and intestines and will help the digestive processes, the breathing, the circulation, and the nerves. And, as improvement is noted, the severity of the exercise may be gradually increased until one is able to take part in the popular sports such as golf, tennis, rowing, swimming, skating, bicycling, etc. In my personal sanitarium activities every patient who can do so secures thirty minutes or more of calisthenic drill once or twice daily. Care must be taken in each case, however, to stop short of the point of actual fatigue, to prevent the accumulation of fatigue poisons in the system.

Of course, for those who can afford it, an automobile trip of an hour or two will be excellent. If the health permits, horseback riding for an hour or two will prove a splendid form of exercise.

HOW A HOPEFUL FRAME OF MIND HELPS

It should go, almost without saying, that a cheerful, contented frame of mind is a decided asset in the ultimate success of any form of treatment.

Under the cheerful influence of hope and

confidence all the normal secretions are increased. Physiological functioning is stimulated. M. Coué has crystallized—or rather resurrected—a great truth when he has given us a formula for focusing the conviction of certain improvement—physically, mentally and socially and financially.

We must learn to tap these hidden subconscious reservoirs for health and energy by assuring ourselves that health and energy are coming to us and that nothing can keep them from coming.

I do not want to be understood in the least as holding that there is not in milk alone, properly taken, all the elements that are needed to build sound, healthy tissue in place of diseased or starved structures. For the milk treatment is not hypnotism or autosuggestion. Its victories do not depend on any mental or suggestive formula.

I do mean, however, that your cure will be greatly hastened if you preserve a cheerful, confident frame of mind and a firm assurance that you are going to get well and strong, and that, despite any temporary setback, the ultimate outcome of your treatment is absolutely certain to be as favorable as your most sanguine expectations.

Nor need you concern yourself with whether your stomach juices are hyper-acid or sub-acid; whether or not you are eliminating the proper balance of urea and uric acid; or whether the blood corpuscles show the increase you expect them to show.

All these things are incidental and have no immediate direct bearing on the ultimate result of your treatment. When you begin to feel better you will *know* it, and no one can tell you the opposite—or, at least, make you believe it. When you start to increase in weight, your scales and your clothes will convey to you this information.

If you feel relaxed and disinclined to exert yourself, so much the better. Try to remember that this is, in all probability, Nature's way of telling you that she is busy building up your tired, wasted body—replacing dead, worn-out cells with new, healthy, vigorous tissue—and that she hopes you'll have sense enough to accept her suggestions to rest up and give her a chance to do her work.

After a day's hard work the body needs the night's rest. After a long period of overwork, illness, or abuse it needs a correspondingly long time to put itself once more in proper functioning shape.

WARM BATHS HELPFUL

One of the most certain and most practical means of helping to secure relaxation is the protracted warm bath—the so-called "neutral bath"—taken at a temperature a few degrees above body heat, or, at most, at a temperature not to exceed 110 degrees Fahrenheit.

The effect of this bath is to soothe the nerves, equalize the circulation, promote a freer excretion through the pores, and cause a general relaxation of all tissues and organs, which puts them into best shape for absorbing nutriment.

The warm bath is not in the slightest degree weakening, as so many erroneously believe, though a hot bath, too long continued,

often has this effect. Indeed, many sorely
wounded soldiers, during the late war, have
been kept in the warm bath for weeks at a
time, eating and sleeping right in the bath,
with head supported by a strap saddle or a
rubber pillow. It is said that two hours'
sleep in the warm bath is equal in recuperative power to an entire night's sleep in bed,
for the relaxation is so much more pronounced, the recuperation from fatigue is so
much more rapid.

I am thoroughly convinced that the daily
warm bath is of the most decided advantage
in bringing about the best results of the milk
treatment. Especially in all conditions char-
acterized by pain and soreness are these baths
valuable, for the uric acid of rheumatism is
eliminated more rapidly, tenderness or inflammation in muscles or joints is relieved,
and a new and better functioning ability is
brought about through the equalization of
pressure on the body surfaces.

If a patient on the milk diet is up and
about, at his regular work or taking consid-

erable exercise, perhaps the best time for his bath would be before his milk in the morning or an hour or two after the milk has been discontinued in the evening.

If one is not working but is taking exercise once a day, this exercise may be taken early in the morning, to be followed by the bath. Or, as with the bedfast patient, milk may be discontinued at one or two periods in the forenoon or afternoon (preferably early afternoon) and the bath taken about thirty minutes after the last glass of milk.

If sufficient time is taken for drying the body and dressing—that is, if these are done leisurely—the milk may be taken immediately after the full completion of the bath.

I do not believe it wise or necessary to use the skin rubbings of oil as an adjunct to the milk treatment. This is chiefly for the reason that the skin organically absorbs but very little oil anyhow, even if oil were needed —which it usually is not.

Further, the oil tends to clog up the orifices of the pores of the skin. This prevents the proper functioning of the sweat glands, and restricts the activity of the eliminating process.

HOW TOBACCO HINDERS THE TREATMENT

I am so thoroughly convinced, as all readers of my book "The Truth About Tobacco" will remember, of the harmfulness of the use of tobacco in health that I can not refrain from condemning it without reserve in all conditions where the health function is distorted.

Many nervous disorders are made infinitely worse by the use of tobacco, particularly by the inhalation of cigarette smoke.

The kidneys, as in Bright's disease, are especially susceptible to the irritating effect of nicotine absorption as they are to the effect of coffee. Therefore I do not believe that any person who continues to smoke or to drink coffee or tea during the course of this treatment is doing either himself or the treatment full justice, particularly as the craving for tobacco, as well as for tea and coffee, will generally cease if only the milk be persistently used for a few days.

AND DON'T READ TOO MUCH

Many people are not content to relax and just rest. They must be occupied every waking moment. If they are not otherwise engaged, they insist upon putting in their time in reading or sewing. Both these occupations use up a certain amount of energy that should be utilized in building up healthy tissue.

Take it easy. If you must read, select some light reading material, and then do not read continuously or feel that you have to finish the book on schedule time. Read only for a few minutes at a time. Then lay the paper or book down until you are impelled to pick it up again.

The same is true of talking. Most talking is unprofitable. If it is a discussion on any deep subject, or any matter that entails much brain activity, it may be a distinct hindrance to early recovery. And much light talk is time-killing, nerve-frazzling, and energy-dissipating. Wait until you are well. Then talk. This will save a lot of vital force and help you to make a quicker and more gratifying recovery.

REFRAIN FROM SEXUAL INDULGENCE

Remember that when the system is below par, and when every effort is being made to bring it up to par, the vital organs should have the most complete rest it is possible to obtain.

With a rapidly assimilated food, such as milk—which contains large quantities of phosphorus and other nerve-stimulating salts —there is not infrequently an unusual tonic influence exerted on the reproductive organs.

However, it would be well not to dissipate any of the precious energy that is needed for the rebuilding of damaged tissue or starved cells by giving way to what might seem perfectly natural impulses for sex gratification.

If the nutriment that goes into the formation of semen and sperm cells is permitted to seek its natural channel, according to the laws of selective affinity, brain and nerve cells will benefit by their conservation.

If you feel you must use up some of the vigor and vital energy that follows the liberal feeding on highly nourishing food, take a walk, or exercise, or occupy your mind in some constructive way. I hope a word to the wise may be sufficient in this respect.

EMERGENCY ALTERNATIVE REGIMENS

By what has already been said in favor of the milk diet, I am sure many people will make sacrifices or so adjust conditions that they can follow this régime for the correction of one or more physical disorders. But there will be some instances where, because of occupation, constant travelling, etc., it will be difficult to follow strictly the full milk diet. Yet many of these people require the milk diet for the correction of their disorders.

Can this diet be modified and still accomplish the same results in these cases? No. At least the same results can not be accomplished in the same length of time. Possibly one will have to be content with only a part of the improvement he might secure were it possible for him to take the regular milk diet.

Without doubt, however, modification of the diet may be used in certain instances with considerable benefit. One of the best alternative treatments is that given in Chapter V for changing from milk to solid food. That is, the milk may be taken the first part of the day and a meal of solid food in the evening. The reverse of this may be used as successfully in some cases—that is, a meal in the morning and the milk from one until seven o'clock.

Another good plan, especially for those who have little or no difficulty in maintaining weight, is to take very slowly a quart of milk for breakfast, one for noon, and one in the evening. If more than this quantity is required, then perhaps a pint may be taken at mid-forenoon, another at mid-afternoon, and another shortly before retiring.

A plan that has been very successful in some cases, especially where milk was desired for a long period of time, is a quart of milk at each of three meals of sweet fruit. For instance, twelve to fifteen dates, or three or four ounces of raisins, or eight to twelve figs may be taken with either sweet milk, sumik, or buttermilk. Or, in place of the fruit there may be taken finely ground whole wheat muffins thoroughly baked. These may be made with raisins or black figs, or some of each. It is better not to use these muffins at each of three meals. Instead, use them at one or two meals, and fruit as above mentioned at the other one or two meals. With this plan it is better to have one meal of milk alone or milk and acid fruit.

If allowance is made for the bulk and the protein element of milk, then milk may be taken at any or all of the three regular meals during the day. It should not be taken with meats or fish, and seldom with nuts or eggs.

So far as I know, there are no chemical or physiological reasons worth considering why milk can not be taken with green salads. These two may constitute the main bulk of a meal, and some whole wheat preparation or sweet fruit may be used at the same time.

The more milk one consumes—within reason—and the more this milk constitutes the main portion of the diet, the more will one be apt to derive the benefits possible on the exclusive milk diet.

Bear in mind that your life and happiness depend upon health. If an accident should befall you, you would be obliged to take time off until correction had been accomplished. If you had some acute illness of a serious nature you would probably be confined for several weeks. In either instance the world would move on just the same. When such a normalizing agent as the milk diet is at your service for correcting disorders of almost any nature and degree, it would be best not to compromise with some modification of the diet, but plan to take the treatment while it would require a comparatively short time to re-establish the proper balance in your physiological activities. You may be saving yourself from serious illness or from a rather protracted course of treatment, with consequent greater loss of time than may now be required.

MILK—THE GREAT HEALTH RESTORER AND PRESERVER

I may be over-enthusiastic about the milk diet, but I believe that the person who knows how to use the fast and milk diet has a regimen at hand that can be adapted to and used successfully in almost any form of acute and chronic ailment. And even should necessity through disease never arise, a short fast followed by a few weeks of milk diet every year will keep any one well, give renewed energy, greater resistance to disease, a cleaner complexion, and a better feeling of bodily comfort than any spring tonic or blood purifier ever compounded.

Perhaps the most eloquent tribute that has ever been paid to milk and to the source from which it is secured is the tribute from Gov. Frank O. Lowden of Illinois, in a pamphlet issued by the Illinois Department of Agriculture: "The cow is a most wonderful laboratory. She takes the grasses of the pasture and the roughage of the field and converts them into the most perfect food

101

for man. In that food there is a mysterious something which scientists have found essential to the highest health of the human race, which can be found nowhere else. Men have sought for centuries the fabled fountain of youth. The nearest approach to that fountain yet discovered is the udder of the cow."

CHAPTER IV

Preventing and Remedying Symptoms, Disturbances and Mishaps During the Milk Diet

TROUBLES FROM ABNORMAL GASTRIC DIGESTION.—
NAUSEA AND VOMITING ON THE MILK DIET.—
LEMON JUICE AS A REMEDY.—THE MILK DIET AND
CONSTIPATION.—CORRECTIVE MEASURES.—DIAR-
RHEA ON MILK DIET.—WHY OLD PAINFUL CONDI-
TIONS AND SYMPTONS SOMETIMES RECUR TEMPO-
RARILY.—ADVICE TO THE CONSUMPTIVE.—ACUTE
DISEASE, TYPHOID, APPENDICITIS.—BLADDER IN-
FLAMMATION.—STONES IN THE KIDNEY OR BLAD-
DER.—MILK AND THE KIDNEYS.—MILK IN WO-
MEN'S DISORDERS.—MILK IN HEART DISEASE.—
THE MILK TREATMENT IN PELLAGRA.—"MILK
REACTION" IN RHEUMATISM.—OTHER SYMPTOMS
ON THE MILK RÉGIME.

THE chief disturbance caused by milk, in using this food drink exclusively in the milk treatment, is brought about most generally by the difficulty of the weakened or otherwise abnormal stomach to take care of the curds and clots formed.

It may be said that the digestion of milk in the food tube differs from that of any other food because of its clotting. The clots formed in the stomach vary greatly, both in size and character.

Sometimes they remain in fine flocculent or feathery masses; sometimes they shrink up into bullet-like lumps; and sometimes they form great tough balls of curd that can hardly be regurgitated, or vomited, back through the oesophagus, the diameter is so great.

It is obvious that the finer and more flocculent the curd, the more readily the gastric juices can attack it and break up the albumin, carrying forward gastric digestion.

Many different methods and expedients, therefore, have been tried in the effort to keep the curds small and soft. And, though my experience has proven that most of these methods are unsatisfactory or even harmful, it may be of interest to the reader to know of them.

Some food authorities and dietitians advise diluting the milk with lime water, milk

of magnesia, or some other alkali. This neu-
tralizes the slight natural acidity of cow's
milk, retards the formation of the curd for
a longer time, and thereby favors the form-
ing of softer and more flocculent curds.
Others again favor the use of some sort of
cereal dilution, such as thin, strained oat-
meal gruel or barley water.

Still others suggest that the milk be boiled
or that the fat content be reduced. Others
advocate the use of some of the peptogenic
ferments to assist in peptonizing the milk and
thereby render it more digestible.

A series of experiments made recently at
the Jefferson Medical College on a human
being who had the faculty of being able to
regurgitate the contents of his stomach at
will has thrown a new light on these questions, although it is more than likely that
they may require considerable verification
before the conclusions arrived at will be
finally accepted, especially when the milk
diet treatment is considered.

Briefly, discarding the test tube and beaker, these experimenters found out that milk drunk rapidly left the stomach sooner and produced a smaller curd mass than milk drunk slowly or "sipped." This is quite as revolutionary as was the now admitted assertion that water drunk at meal time is not an unmixed evil, or that the "fletcherizing" of food fails to accomplish any marvels in digestion, but it is one idea that can never be adopted in the milk cure.

Again, it is learned that raw cow's milk forms a large, hard curd, whereas boiled milk curds in a much finer and softer form; that the presence of much cream (milk fat) in the milk insures the formation of particularly soft curds which are slow to leave the stomach; that skimmed milk yields a particularly hard curd, owing to the absence of fat; that pasteurized milk shows smaller curds than the raw whole milk, but larger than the boiled whole milk, and finally that cold milk coagulates more slowly than warm milk.

Some of these finds had been previously known — some were rather revolutionary.

The broad fact must be considered, however, that what may apply to the digestion of milk in this one particular instance is no proof of its universal applicability. I should fear to adopt some of the suggested procedures when applying the exclusive milk diet.

Stomachs and digestive apparatus vary quite as much as do the owners of these digestive organs, and, in the final analysis, good judgment and personal experience will have to decide intimate questions of diet. But experience in thousands of cases has given me an opportunity to learn the many exceptions to a normal digestion of the milk and the most appropriate treatment in these cases. Suffice it to say that, in this wide experience, I have found boiled milk totally unsatisfactory in all but rare cases, and that rapid drinking of milk is always detrimental when on an exclusive milk diet.

NAUSEA AND VOMITING FROM THE MILK DIET

Many people, on commencing the milk diet, become quite nauseated. The stomach rebels. This often results from trying to "wade" too quickly into the milk cure and is often entirely overcome if the full amount of milk is taken on schedule time from the very start of the treatment.

The "bad" stomach is often in such a condition that its so-called warnings may be very safely disregarded, for it doesn't know what's good for itself or the body for which it has to help prepare nourishment. It has been misused and abused for so long that all it is willing to do is to pass along some pre-digested material that doesn't require any great expenditure of energy for it to get rid of and that may furnish only a small amount of vitality to the body anyhow.

It is well to give the stomach some real work to do, or something that will make rich, red blood and build strength and vitality into the system. After a few days of struggle the new circulation, filling the arteries and veins and bathing every cell in its nutrient juices, will stimulate the glands and the cells to produce their own digestive juices. Then the nausea and the sickness will stop and all will be well.

MISHAPS DURING MILK DIET

A small percentage of people in taking the milk diet will have a nausea that is more or less disturbing, and that continuous drinking of straight milk will not correct. It is sometimes of a short duration, terminating automatically, but in some instances this condition steadily increases with each additional glass of milk taken until the individual is apt to discontinue the milk entirely, or until the nausea is increased to the point where it produces a vomiting of the stomach contents. Rarely is it necessary for these individuals to be disturbed in this way.

Sometimes it will be found that they have been taking milk too rich in butter fat, and merely skimming off all or most of the cream will allay the nausea. However, there is one simple remedy that will prove effective in perhaps ninety-nine per cent of the cases. This remedy is lemon juice.

LEMON JUICE AN EFFECTIVE REMEDY

Some patients carry a lemon in a paper napkin so as to have it with them at all times. A small hole may be cut in one end, and after occasional glasses of milk, or after every glass if necessary, a few drops of lemon juice may be taken.

In some instances it may be taken immediately before the milk, but usually taking it directly after the milk will prove more effective.

A lemon may be cut in small sections, say into eighths, and one of these used after every glass of milk. It is better to take the juice directly from the lemon than to have the juice squeezed out and taken from a glass.

How much lemon juice will be required in any individual case is difficult to say. Sometimes as little as one-quarter of a lemon a day will be sufficient; on the other hand, one patient I recall required one lemon with each pint of milk taken, and as he took twelve pints daily, he was using twelve lemons. This is probably the largest amount that has ever been required.

Many people will not require lemon juice at all, but those who do will rarely require more than one or two lemons a day.

If, as may rarely happen, this does not allay the trouble, discontinue the milk and all food but hot water until the stomach is empty and a desire for milk is noticeable. Then, preparatory to beginning again, take a small amount of lemon juice, or one half hour before time for the milk take the juice of an orange or half a grape fruit.

After a few weeks of the treatment in at least seventy-five per cent of the cases there is apt to be a steadily increasing nausea or a condition where the milk is distasteful, and where this lack of desire for the milk can not be corrected by lemon juice, skimmed milk, or other simple procedures. In these cases, practically without exception, the body has made as much improvement as possible without further fasting or without a change of diet. This condition usually appears after five or six weeks of the diet. It would usually be satisfactory to take a fast, the length of which will depend upon its effects, and to return again to the milk diet for further improvement. The system seems to be more eager for the milk on the second or following attempts or after a brief respite from the diet, and the improvement will then be more marked.

If for any reason this diet can not be continued longer than when this condition of dislike for the milk develops (usually after five to seven weeks of the diet), it will be well to return to solid food as described in Chapter V.

Those of the "bilious type," who have over-active livers and an excess of bile, occasionally have an uncontrollable vomiting— usually on the fast, if at all, but sometimes on the milk diet. This may begin at any time during the milk diet, but usually not for a few weeks after beginning. The milk should be discontinued promptly and a large amount of water taken. This may have the effect of carrying the contents of the stomach and upper intestines further down in the intestines and thus flushing the digestive tract. If it does not do this, it will dilute the bile and gastric secretions so that they will be easily expelled from the stomach and, at the same time, be less acrid and irritating.

This condition is usually brought on by too much cream; by taking the milk too cold; too large quantities at a time; or taking drinks too close together; or as a "healing crisis." It may continue for two, three or four days, but it is not apt to do this if the stomach is flushed immediately. The use of lemon juice here is also very valuable, either to allay the nausea and vomiting somewhat, or after the stomach has been emptied of all milk residue.

In some instances, especially in cases of kidney trouble, liver trouble, and prolapsus or dilation of the stomach, this nausea may be present only (or practically only) upon exertion or upon assuming the upright position. Consequently, merely resuming or assuming the reclining posture will allay the symptom. In some few other cases of stomach abnormality vomiting may occur only upon reclining, especially on the left side. Changing position or assuming the half-sitting, half-reclining posture will usually correct this tendency.

In the summer-time if one is very hot

(usually from undue exertion), or if one has been exercising, one may take the milk before sufficiently cooling, or too soon after the exertion, and may have a nausea and probably vomiting with or without severe gastric pains. Avoid this condition by being careful to have the system prepared for the milk when it is taken. But if you have been indiscreet in this manner, do not take the milk until the symptom has subsided, and hasten the relief by drinking hot water or using lemon juice, or both; and probably by the use of hot abdominal packs, if the trouble is considerable and obstinate.

FURTHER SUGGESTIONS REGARDING
LEMON JUICE

It is best always to begin the use of lemon immediately on the slightest indication of nausea. Do not wait until the condition is well developed. Take as many lemons as necessary, but as few as possible to correct the disturbance. If lemon appears to be too acid, an excellent plan is to mix orange and lemon juices, or grapefruit may be used in some few instances.

Have no fear of any harmful results from combining milk and acid fruits, regardless of theories and teachings along this line. In practically every case lemon can be used without fear of any trouble.

In rare instances, however, it is found that lemon itself will produce a nausea. If it does, then sweet fruits such as dates, particularly, or figs, or raisins, and sometimes a small amount of honey, may prove satisfactory, but one should never take sugar, as the trouble will be aggravated by this. The need for sweet fruit and honey will be extremely rare, and when apparently required they must be taken in the smallest amount possible to accomplish their purpose.

Except in cases so rare that it might be safe to say, in no case, should any other articles of food be taken with the milk except fruit, and never even this unless for the purpose of correcting some unnatural condition. However, when using pasteurized milk, acid fruit juice should be taken in addition.

Sometimes the milk will be better taken
care of if sucked through a straw with an
opening so small that it may require an
effort to draw the milk into the mouth. This
sucking method brings about a better mix-
ing of the saliva with the milk and in some
cases may aid in its digestion. At least the
milk is more apt to enter the stomach in
smaller amounts. But be sure to keep the
milk well mixed by shaking or stirring, if
this method is employed, so as not to have
too rich milk toward the end of the bottle.

My own method, as previously stated, is
to press my lips over the glass and make the
opening so small that it is necessary to suck
in the milk just as would a suckling baby.

At other times it is helpful to aerate the
milk, pouring it from one glass into the other
until there is a good froth on the surface of
the milk. This prevents, to a certain degree,
the rapid formation of hard curds.

Many doctors and food experts who look
unfavorably upon milk as a curative diet
have contended that the stomach rebels because it is constantly at work and that it

needs a period of rest, which, of course, it does not get during the daytime when milk is taken regularly at half hour intervals. This is true in connection with the use of all ordinary foods, or even with milk itself, if taken in connection with other food. However, when there is nothing except milk (with fruit juices, when indicated, as mentioned) taken into the stomach, there is not, in my experience, any harm in adding more milk.

In fact, the partly digested milk acts as a "starter" for the new supply, combining with it perfectly. The practical experience of thousands of people who have taken milk in this manner, with the best of results, confirms this.

It might be mentioned here that practically all slight digestive troubles of the stomach that develop on the milk diet will almost invariably be corrected by the use of lemon juice. These troubles may be a fullness or bloating, more or less pain or distress, and acid regurgitation into the throat or mouth, a "turning against milk," etc.

THE MILK DIET AND CONSTIPATION

Many people have taken and will take the milk diet for the correction of a chronic condition of constipation. Past experience has shown that, while this diet is corrective, it is not so in the same way that drug laxatives, bran, oils, etc., are corrective. Instead it is corrective because of its normalizing and re-educative effects.

However, constipation is one of the symptoms that is apt to develop where the milk diet is taken, regardless of the original condition for which it is taken.

Many patients believe that when constipation develops on this diet they will fail to secure beneficial results otherwise, and that the constipation may be more or less permanent. If the diet has been prepared for, if it is taken properly, and if it is broken from correctly, no permanent constipation will be developed.

If laxatives of any nature have been taken previous to starting on the milk diet there will, of course, be a withdrawal of these stimulating agents. As is the case when formerly-used stimulants are avoided, there is a reaction toward lessened activity. If bran and such substances that secure effect through mechanical means have been used, the nerve endings have no such stimulants in milk residue to excite activity. If drug laxatives have been employed, the secretions and structures of the digestive canal are freed from the need of increased activity in order to expel these poisons from the system (which is the action secured to accomplish results with this form of laxative), and because they have already been over-stimulated their action will be materially lessened.

If oils have formerly been used, the milk diet leaves no similar lubricating material, and constipation may result. The intestinal activity may be so retarded, and the nerves of the lower colon and rectum so unresponsive to the mild stimulation given by the marble-like smoothness of the milk residue, that this residue is retained unduly long and until all the moisture has been absorbed. This frequently leaves the rectal contents exceptionally dry or very large. In either case this will delay bowel action.

To correct temporarily this trouble when on the milk diet the enema has proven by far the most valuable means. A pint of cool water is usually all that is necessary to stimulate the rectum to discharge its waste. It may be necessary to repeat this immediately. Avoid larger amounts if possible, as they will have a tendency to dissolve the rectal contents, from which may be absorbed some toxic elements more or less harmful to the system.

In cases where exercise is permissible, walking, various abdominal movements, particularly the retraction of the abdomen, or massage, early in the morning or sometime after the last milk in the evening may prove effective. Or at these times "cannon ball" massage may be employed.

This latter massage is given by means of a croquet or similar ball rolled over the abdomen from the lower right-hand corner up to the ribs, across to the left side, down to the lower left-hand corner, and across to the starting point. One or more garments may be between the flesh and the ball.

If the milk diet is taken for some other condition than digestive—if there has been absolutely no disorder of the digestive tract —after the first three or four weeks of straight milk one may eat from four to six prunes, taking that amount once, twice, or three times daily if still constipated. These prunes should be soaked and not cooked. In a few such cases a small amount of figs may be used, but these have more of a tendency to produce gas and bloating; also they are more mechanically stimulating, and may cause more or less irritation.

In some instances of constipation and paradoxically, in other instances of diarrhea, agar-agar (Japanese Seaweed) may be used with benefit. I believe it would be best, however, to avoid the use of anything that has no definite food value. We rarely recommend sand for constipation.

Oils interfere with the digestion and absorption of milk and should not be used. In fact, some cases of constipation are corrected by removing some of the cream. In the majority of instances, however, whole milk will be better in cases of constipation unless there are contra-indications for its use, as given in Chapter II or Chapter IV.

In not a few cases, however, we have found that sumik or buttermilk taken according to the regular milk diet régime will re-establish normal bowel activity. It may be necessary to take only a few glasses a day of either of these, while using mainly the sweet milk; or either may be taken throughout the day or even throughout the milk diet régime.

In some other instances, taking the milk cooler or considerably warmer may be satisfactory, in which case usually only a glass or two of this milk of altered temperature may be required. If a very few glasses do not accomplish the result it will probably prove ineffective to take it in larger amounts.

If the use of one or two oranges a few minutes before the first milk in the morning, and the simple abdominal exercises and walking do not produce the desired correction of constipation, then resort to the enema, and do not fear to use it regularly—throughout the course of the milk diet if necessary.

Many cases of constipation developing on the milk diet, if not corrected by continuation of the diet, will disappear spontaneously when the regular diet is resumed. Do not return to this diet, however, unless results desired in other respects from the milk diet have been secured.

The best results in practically every case are more apt to be secured where the milk diet is taken "straight"—without the addition of anything solid; but, when necessary, with acid fruit juices, and always the enema when indicated.

DIARRHEA SOMETIMES MORE TROUBLESOME THAN CONSTIPATION

The opposite condition of bowel activity less frequently interferes when on the milk diet. However, diarrhea may develop and must be considered. Usually this should not be interfered with in any way for two or

three days. It may be a necessary house-
cleaning that will subside naturally by the
end of this time. If not, and it is weakening
in effect, steps may be taken to control it
somewhat.

Skimmed milk rarely causes this condition, and should be the first method employed for its correction. If this is not
effective, reducing the quantity of milk to
one-half, or dispensing with the milk entirely until the diarrhea has subsided may be
resorted to, and then the amount gradually
increased while the intestinal tolerance is
being carefully observed.

Sometimes diluting the milk with plain
water, with lime water, or barley water may
be used effectively. Use as small amount of
these waters as necessary. This may be one
or two ounces or more to each eight-ounce
glass of milk.

Also a teaspoonful or more of malted
milk, well dissolved into each glass of milk
necessary, has been used satisfactorily. In
this condition lowering the temperature of
the milk has sometimes proved satisfactory.

Rarely will increasing the temperature of the milk have the desired effect.

In the majority of cases, perhaps, maintaining the recumbent posture will be all that is necessary. In a considerable number of cases, however, this can not be followed strictly enough, and one of the other plans given may be necessary.

While sumik and buttermilk are usually more laxative in effect, it has sometimes been observed that they will check diarrhea. At least they may be tried if desired or necessary.

If no digestive or intestinal troubles existed before beginning the milk—if there is no particular irritation or weakness of the stomach or intestines—dates may be given usually with fully satisfactory results in cases of diarrhea, after a few weeks of the strict milk diet. From one to four dates may be used with each glass of milk, though the smallest number possible for effect should be used, and with as few glasses of milk during the day as possible for results.

Sometimes diarrhea will develop as a

"healing crisis" after several weeks of the milk régime. In these cases, the fast is positively indicated and should continue until this symptom and any other that may have developed at the same time have subsided.

WHY OLD PAINFUL CONDITIONS SOMETIMES RETURN

It has been noted by many who have taken the milk treatment that painful conditions, such as rheumatism, headache, backache, skin eruptions, and sometimes a dull "stretching" pain in the kidneys, stomach, liver and other organs, and numerous old time symptoms seem to develop.

Occasionally there is a slight return of earache, or a pain at the seat of any old inflammatory process that has affected the lungs, the pleura, the intestinal wall, or the mucous membrane lining of the generative organs, especially if there are any evidences of adhesions or stricture present.

In ovarian or uterine irritation, especially about the time of the menstrual flow, this pain is often quite pronounced.

I should like to impress strongly on the minds of those suffering from these symptoms that, while stopping the milk will relieve these pains, as a rule it would be better to "grin and bear it" for a while.

For the pain is merely an indication that Nature is active in building new capillaries and blood vessels in this old disused tissue, or that it is stretching out and strengthening fibrous tissues and sensitive coverings of organs or the peritoneal lining of the abdomen, and building new cells and putting new life into cells that have become partially atrophied by disease and more or less paralyzed in their functions.

It is really a condition of "growing pains" applied to local areas that are but transitory in their nature. The pain must be accepted only as an indication of physiological activity and repair in these areas.

When on the milk diet some few symptoms that are new to the patient may arise, but these are usually insignificant and occasion no alarm. But the old symptoms returning are apt to lead the patient to believe that the milk is causing a return of the very condition for which the milk is taken. In the healing process it is only natural to expect that, as the formerly diseased and abnormal structures are undergoing alteration, symptoms relative to them and symptoms which have been experienced before will become manifest.

An irritation of a certain nerve will produce a certain symptom or reaction, whether that irritation is of a depressive, inflammatory, or toxic nature, or in the process of stimulation to normal activity by a natural régime.

Drug doctors and surgeons know nothing of this "retracing of symptoms" or "healing crisis," or "repair changes," that are frequently met with in drugless treatment. For their methods of treatment are suppressive, and do not give the various abnormal organs, tissues and structures an opportunity to "retrace" from an existing condition back through the different phases of abnormality to health and normal functioning.

The physical culture régime, and especially the milk diet régime, aids nature in establishing or re-establishing normal from abnormal conditions, and when these old symptoms reappear they should be welcomed rather than otherwise, as one can then feel that he is "back-tracking" over the route by which he arrived at his low state of health and his diseased condition.

So far as they may be responsible for or indicative of actual harmful effects, I can only repeat that, in an experience with hundreds upon hundreds of every conceivable sort of chronic trouble—from headache to syphilis—I have seen instances of the most remarkable improvement where these symptoms have been most severe, and that I have never seen any real damage or permanent harm done by the milk treatment. The only cases in which it might be actually dangerous to "push" the treatment are those cases associated with hemorrhage, or where there is a tendency toward apoplexy.

Some object to milk in diseases of a catarrhal nature, saying that it increases mucous discharge. It is true that such discharges increase in the beginning of the milk diet, but this is due to the increased circulation of blood to all parts of the body, and to the fact that the system is literally cleansing itself of waste matter; and when this is effected the catarrhal discharges will cease—not before.

When one has been feeding upon foods of an acid-forming nature, such as beef, bacon, eggs, white flour products, oatmeal, polished rice, etc., and the symptoms of an acid toxemia are present, milk will very quickly relieve the conditions, as it has an excess of basic or alkaline-forming elements.

Catarrh could never exist in any system if the normal eliminative organs were acting normally, or if while acting normally they could remove all of the toxic elements and excess waste materials that we are constantly taking into and producing in our systems.

Since the normal eliminative organs can

not keep the body freed from undesirable elements, the mucous membrane is called into use to assist them, but this elimination is really vicarious—a substitute in case of need.

Catarrh is merely a house-cleaning effort on the part of the human economy, regardless of where the catarrh exists. This may be in the nose and throat, in the stomach, intestines, bladder, or wherever there is mucous membrane.

It is true that more or less severe chronic catarrhal conditions may develop, but that is not because catarrh itself is a disease—merely that waste elements have been formed in such abundance, and have been thrown out in such large amounts through the mucous membrane, that a low form of inflammation has developed.

As the milk diet is healing for any structure of the body, and as old symptoms are returned, or present symptoms temporarily aggravated, it is only natural to expect that catarrhal discharge, directly, an eliminative effort, will be increased.

ADVICE TO THE CONSUMPTIVE

While from four to six weeks' treatment usually suffices for the relief or permanent cure of very many disorders, it is obvious that this happy result can not be hoped for so speedily in tuberculosis—as well as in several other diseases.

The treatment of tuberculosis is a campaign, not a battle, and must be fought out in some cases for years, instead of months, and in any case for many months.

Also, there are many contributing factors —such as climate, exercise and fresh air, freedom from anxiety and economic worries —that must be taken into consideration and planned for.

Also remember it is not wise to place too much importance upon mere increase in weight. The condition of the blood must be improved, and this vital fluid once more given the proper building power and resistance to disease processes. The progress of the lung condition (or the bone condition, in the case of tubercular spine or hip, or of whatever tissue or organ affected) will then be arrested, and the patient turned up-hill toward health and life.

Remember also that, almost invariably, there is temporarily when on the milk diet a considerable increase in the amount of expectoration. Often there is even a distressing increase in the cough itself. These symptoms, however, merely show a greater activity on the part of the lung cells in throwing off consolidated portions of the lung tissue which have been loosened up by the curative effects of the milk. It means that the air is entering more and more of the pulmonary cells which have hitherto been filled up with broken down products of the degenerative process.

Most generally the cough is easy and the expectoration is much more free — where formerly the cough was hard and racking and the material voided with extreme difficulty.

Later on, of course, both the cough and the expectoration are decreased, and air can be heard entering lung areas that were formerly quite consolidated.

I can not emphasize too strongly the inestimable value of fresh air, day and night —and every day and every night—to anyone afflicted with tuberculosis.

TEETH DO NOT DECAY BECAUSE OF THE MILK DIET

It is frequently alleged that the exclusive milk diet tends to cause decay and softening of the teeth, the formation of cavities, the development of pyorrhea, and, occasionally, even the loss of one or more teeth.

This is perfectly absurd. For milk is extremely rich in lime and other mineral salts that go to build up tooth structure. It is, in fact, one of the best foods that could be taken by any one who wanted to secure the best possible nutriment for tooth and bone development.

However, a protracted fast, taken before beginning the milk treatment, may sometimes cause the appearance of cavities in the teeth. This is for the reason that when no food is taken, there may be a tendency on the part of the system to abstract the lime salts from the teeth, in order to maintain the normal alkalinity of the blood, or to provide the vital stimulating food for various of the ductless glands, which depend almost entirely upon the presence of calcium salts for stimulus to their normal functioning.

Or, some people may take but two or three quarts of milk a day—perhaps less than half of what they need to give them the full food requirements.

The solution of both these problems is simple. In the one instance it suggests that the period of fasting be limited to a day or two at most, particularly in the case of under-nourished, emaciated individuals, or that the fast be made a fruit fast. In the other case, that they go on a *full* milk diet—a glass of milk every half hour—every hour they are awake, up to twelve to fourteen hours.

This will prevent the loss of nutrient salts for the teeth, and the drain on their structure that results in the formation of cavities.

For the benefit of those who may entertain any doubt whatsoever on this subject, I would say that I have known many people who have been constantly under the care of their dentist for reparative work on their teeth, who, after inaugurating a course of diet in which ample supplies of milk were an integral part, never again had the slightest trouble with cavity formation in their teeth. And this for the reasons above stated.

DILATED STOMACH MAY REQUIRE SPECIAL MODIFICATION IN MILK RÉGIME

Many have contended that the use of large quantities of fluid is necessarily contra-indicated where there already exists a dilated condition of the stomach.

The argument is advanced that in these cases the diet should be concentrated and of the lightest possible character.

In one way they are right. If you drink full quantities of milk, and remain at work or on the feet a greater part of the time, it will be quite impossible by this treatment to restore the stomach once more to its normal position and dimensions.

However, to prevent this contingency is comparatively simple. It merely requires that you should go to bed, or take a complete rest at least. If a full milk diet is taken, under conditions of perfect rest, there will be little or no difficulty in restoring tone to the weakened, relaxed walls of the stomach, and strengthening the muscles and supports of this organ so that it will once more return to its normal size and position.

Where this, the most satisfactory plan, is not possible to follow, then just sufficient milk should be taken to allow a very slow gain in weight without "overloading" the stomach. This amount will vary, naturally, and may be from three to five quarts daily. But it must not be forgotten that the *fast* is of tremendous importance in these cases. I have known dilated stomachs to be returned to normal by the fast alone. But the milk diet is usually necessary to maintain these good results, by supplying requisite reconstructive elements to blood and tissues.

ACUTE DISEASES, TYPHOID AND APPENDICITIS

I believe that in all acute conditions Nature demands perfect rest. Particularly in typhoid, appendicitis, or inflammation of the bowels, it is desirable that no food of any form whatever be given.

In chronic appendical conditions, or in chronic, sub-acute, or catarrhal inflammation of the bowels, the milk treatment has been particularly effective.

In chronic cases of cystitis there are usually thickened bladder walls and degenerated mucous linings which leave a bladder of relatively small capacity. This makes urination quite frequent even on an ordinary diet. For this reason this condition is not infrequently troublesome on the milk diet. Also, if there is much inflammation of the neck of the bladder, it is likely to be quite painful—an act that one would not care to perform any oftener than absolutely necessary.

Yet the chief reason for this pain in urinating is the presence of highly irritating ammoniacal urine, which causes distressing irritation when passing over the delicate and inflamed mucous surfaces at the neck of the bladder. When the amount of urine is increased several times, and the bladder symptoms remain practically the same, it necessarily takes considerable courage and determination to persist in the milk course.

Yet if one who suffers from bladder trouble will but persist in the treatment, it is perfectly astounding how rapidly the highly irritating, scalding urine changes in character to a bland, soothing fluid, free from fetid, decomposing odor, that tends to relieve the lining membrane by its "softness" and freedom from all irritating elements.

This same solvent effect is exercised in the presence of stone in the bladder or kidney, or in ordinary conditions of gravel. There are very few of these cases in which an astonishing degree of improvement is not manifested after a few weeks of conscientious treatment.

MILK AND THE KIDNEYS

It is generally taught by the medical profession that in kidney disease the quantity of fluid should be greatly restricted, "to give the kidney cells a rest."

Experience in hundreds of cases proves this dictum wrong, and even medical doctors are realizing this more and more. For the excessive amount of fluid voided by the kidneys stimulates the organs to resume their natural function — which is to strain out poisons from the blood, and eliminate them from the system.

The urine of even the healthiest people is waste material, and injurious to health unless normally eliminated from the system. Where the kidney cells are damaged and the function of straining these poisons from the blood is inadequately performed, the skin and the bowels are obliged to work beyond their physiological powers.

Where the urine is vastly increased in amount, the toxic material and the waste matter are greatly diluted by the additional amount of water, and most generally a larger total amount of solids is excreted in the urine. This makes elimination easier, and it also tends to purify the blood more rapidly, and thereby remove from the system the chief predisposing cause of the trouble—retained toxic material.

And right here I may say that "floating" or prolapsed kidneys are almost invariably benefited by a milk course. Persistent treatment, maintained for a period of a month or six weeks, will usually restore them to their normal condition.

Kidneys lose their anchorage because of a reduction of their supporting omental (peritoneal or abdominal) fat. Strains, jars, twists and turns, etc., may be the exciting cause of a prolapsus of these organs, but such would be ineffective were it not for the weakening or reduction of supporting tissue. The milk diet supplies cells to any tissue according to the nature and demands of that tissue. When fat is deficient, then through the nourishment by the milk diet fat cells are formed, and in this instance a normal support of kidney fat will be established and the kidneys supported in their normal position.

It is well to mention here the value of utilizing the force of gravity to assist in reducing prolapsed kidneys, or other abdominal or pelvic organs. Elevating the foot of the bed from four to six inches so that gravity may work during sleep is a valuable aid. Other aids that may be mentioned and strongly recommended are: walking on all fours, or assuming a position head downward, preferably upon the back, on an ironing board or similar support, one end of which is on the floor and the other on the side of the bed or chair. Lying on the bed with the hips greatly elevated is similar in effect.

MILK IN WOMEN'S DISORDERS

I have already spoken of the favorable influence of the milk diet in menstrual and other disorders peculiar to women. I should like to emphasize here, however, that in chronic inflammatory conditions of the uterus or ovaries, the acute pain, due to the presence of an extra amount of blood, is always present at the menstrual period.

Therefore, it is good practice to start the milk treatment directly the menses have ceased—fasting during, or before and during the period. Keep up the treatment for three weeks, and then discontinue (fast or fruit fast) until after the cessation of the next period. This will obviate the acute pain that frequently accompanies an increase in the amount of fluid circulating in the blood vessels, and thereby prevent "pressure pains."

If, however, the woman can endure the discomfort of taking the milk right through the period, it is always wise to continue the treatment uninterruptedly, with almost every assurance that at the next period the condition will have materially improved.

The effect is more or less similar to that of a normal labor, which quite frequently brings about a fairly normal pelvic condition, at least so far as menstrual irregularities are concerned.

Some people whose skin is very delicate tend to develop pimples and boils when on the full milk diet. This they may ascribe to an excess of nutriment, and in some instances it is quite likely they may be right. Personally, however, I am of the opinion that the trouble originates chiefly in an increased eliminative effort of the system, plus usually defective elimination from the bowels. When on the milk diet two or even three daily evacuations should be secured if possible to facilitate the removal of toxic matter from the system.

This can best be accomplished by the free use of orange juice, one or two oranges being taken fifteen minutes before the first milk in the morning, and a tablespoonful or more of juice being taken fifteen minutes after the milk, for three or four feedings.

In addition to this, a high enema of a quart of warm water should be taken each night. This should be taken in the knee-chest position—kneeling on a rug or bath-

144

mat or on the bathroom floor, the hips elevated and the left shoulder lowered to the floor.
This facilitates the flow of water up beyond
the sigmoid flexure, and its passage along
the transverse colon. When finally voided,
this water often brings away old scyballæ, or
adherent masses of fecal matter, that have
attached themselves to the bowel surfaces.
The poisons from these semi-dried masses
are absorbed into the circulation. The result
is the disfiguring condition of the skin, manifested in pimples and in skin eruptions.

An occasional dose of castor oil may also
aid in sweeping the accumulated poisons of
intestinal decomposition out of the intestine,
besides putting the entire canal in a better
functioning condition, though this is rarely
advised.

In addition to active elimination, however,
it might be well to reduce the fat content of
the milk. For, when there is any excess of
fat in the dietary, it may require active exercise in the open air to oxidize and completely utilize it.

For this reason, "low fat content milk"

or skim milk should be used instead of whole milk—especially where there is any tendency toward skin eruption.

THE MILK DIET IN HEART DISEASE

Most physicians will say that in the severe forms of heart disease, complicated by leaky valves or failure in the normal compensation, any additional strain on the heart, through increasing the amount of the circulatory fluid, is decidedly to be avoided.

Superficially considered, this might seem to have some elements of sense in it, as the indications are for the most perfect possible rest for the damaged organ. This does not mean to imply that a heart in a damaged state or a ruptured valve can be cured by a course of milk treatment.

Yet the increased amount of nutrition secured from the full milk diet actually tends to restore compensation, and bring about a condition in which the patient may live in comparative comfort for many years.

In those cases, however, in which the chief cause of the "murmur" or the irregularity is anemia, or general debility, or nervous exhaustion, perfect heart function can quite frequently be restored.

Where there is poor circulation, with a sallow, pasty skin, where the individual lacks strength and endurance, or where the typical "anemic murmur" may have developed, a few days' faithful treatment will usually suffice to bring about an astounding degree of improvement—not alone in increasing the strength and vigor of the heart, but also in a gratifying increase in the general health.

THE MILK TREATMENT IN PELLAGRA

The rapid increase of pellagra in the South has directed much discussion to its probable cause, and to the most likely method of curing this serious and often fatal disorder.

Whether the condition be a "deficiency disorder" due to lack of protein and vitamines, or whether it be of germ origin, has not been definitely determined.

My personal opinion is that it is due to dietetic deficiencies, and it is the consensus of opinion that, whatever the cause, the most successful, in fact, the only successful treatment is dietary.

In the New York *Medical Journal,* May 1, 1915, Dr. S. H. Ensminger states regarding diet for pellagra: "In all cases milk should be given if possible. The most important feature of the whole subject is rest."

There is no doubt in mind that the cases reported which did not respond successfully to the milk treatment simply did not get their milk the *proper way.* This is: one glass, or eight ounces, every half hour while awake—taking an average of twenty glasses each day.

In my opinion if this treatment could be given it would cure practically every pellagric in the world. But the poor victims can't get the milk that would save their lives, for there is little or no fresh milk to be had in the pellagrous regions.

THE "MILK REACTION" IN RHEUMATISM

One of the most pronounced reactions following the inauguration of the milk treatment is found in rheumatic or painful joint or muscle-sheath conditions. Usually, a few days after starting treatment, there is a definite return of the old symptoms, the pain most generally appearing in the area in which it originally manifested itself.

If the patient persists in the treatment, paying no attention to the return of his pain, the attack usually disappears within forty-eight hours or so. Within a few days a second attack may come, but less pronounced than the first, and lasting only a short time, and so on.

The reason these "crises" manifest themselves is that the circulation is greatly increased, while yet the blood is loaded with toxins.

The excessive amount of lactic or uric acid —or whatever the product of mal-metabolism that causes rheumatism—is forced by the increased circulation into the tissues in which the circulation had previously been rather sluggish.

Another reason is that the diluted blood tends to re-absorb these toxic elements, and

149

in the process causes an irritation of the originally affected nerves, with old pains.

Remember, the eradication of the poisons of rheumatism by the exclusive milk diet is not the matter of a day or a week. It may take a month or several months.

For the improvement follows because of the fact that milk lacks the elements out of which the poisons of rheumatism are made. It further aids by correcting the depraved processes of digestion, metabolism and elimination that favor the accumulation of the rheumatic toxins in the blood.

Bear in mind that milk is absolutely free from the purin bodies that go to form uric acid, which are found so plentifully in meat, eggs, fish, coffee, tea and cocoa, and which are factors in the development of rheumatic and gouty conditions.

Dr. Sherman, of Columbia University, in commenting on this fact, says: "Milk has the advantage of not containing the substances which yield uric acid to the body."

Arthritis, particularly if of gonorrheal origin, may refuse to yield to the milk treatment, and may require baking of the knee or areas involved, or other forms of special treatment. But this is somewhat outside of the scope of the present work. However, the worst case I ever saw—a "stretcher case"— received complete cure by a "finish fast" of fifty-four days, and six weeks of milk diet.

OTHER SYMPTOMS OF THE MILK RÉGIME

Various other symptoms may arise while one is taking milk, such as headache, backache, pains in the limbs, feeling of weakness and lethargy, or sleeplessness. The rule is to take no notice of these unless fever accompanies them. Fasting is then indicated, the milk being resumed when the acute attack subsides. All the symptoms manifested are indications of the house-cleaning and rejuvenation which the body is undergoing, and are no sign that the milk should be discontinued.

In may cases patients will be able to take the milk diet without a return of any symptoms, or without any apparently adverse developments. They will progress steadily in overcoming the specific condition or conditions for which the milk is taken, until their health is restored to normal.

They may be considered as fortunate individuals, but usually where this steady progression is possible there is not the severe physical abnormality that is present in those cases that do have more or less troubling symptoms.

Where these symptoms develop, I believe the individual can consider himself extremely fortunate also, for it shows that the milk diet is not only producing a favorable reaction in the system, but that the vitality of the body is sufficient to bring about this reaction with the proper aid. While such symptoms may not develop in some individuals with great vitality, rest assured that they will not develop where the vitality has been lowered to the point from which there is no return. Also be assured that there is no other régime that will bring these symptoms and the returning health they indicate more quickly, and yet with less severity than will the milk diet.

When these symptoms develop, the diet usually should be continued steadily and without interruption, unless their appearance is at or about the sixth week (say from five to seven weeks). If they develop at this time, a fast is in order and this may continue for a few days only, or it may be a "finish" fast, and the milk diet should be resumed at its completion.

The only exception, perhaps, to this rule is in case fever develops. In this instance the fast should be instituted at once and continued until the temperature is normal, and, for safety's sake (usually), for a day or so longer.

By following this plan the body will be purified, rejuvenated and restored to a higher degree of health that will be permanent so long as the mode of living is such as to preserve normal functioning activity.

We have in the milk diet, without doubt, the most powerfully effective of all agents for the eradication of poisons, toxins, waste, and unnatural elements of any nature; and for the restoration to normal of any tissue and function capable of restoration; and for removing all obstacles to the highest manifestation of the vital force within the body. No other single food can compare with it, and, for many disorders, no combinations of foods can equal it for effectiveness.

CHAPTER V

How to Change from the Milk Diet

WHY SOME PEOPLE FAIL WITH THE MILK DIET.—BEST
WAY TO DISCONTINUE THE MILK.—"PART-TIME"
MILK DIET PREFERABLE.—COMBINATION MILK AND
ONE MEAL PLAN.—SKIMMED MILK SOMETIMES
BEST.—WATER, FRUIT JUICES, OR MILK SHOULD
FURNISH SUFFICIENT FLUID.—AVOID AUTO-INTOX-
ICATION AND CONSTIPATION.—TELLTALE SYMP-
TOMS OF DEVELOPING AUTO-INTOXICATION.—
PROPER RÉGIME FOR CORRECTING OR PREVENTING
CONSTIPATION.—LACTIC ACID MILK MAY BE USED.
—THE RIGHT KIND OF FOOD.—FOODS TO USE AND
FOODS TO AVOID.—GOITRE CASES REQUIRE CARE.—
WEIGHT GAINED.—SELECTION OF NATIONAL RÉ-
GIME NECESSARY FOR CONTINUING BEST RESULTS.

IN changing from the milk diet back to the
regular diet great care must be exercised,
even though a cure has been established or
great improvement secured.

Many fail to make the benefits of the milk
diet lasting because they make the change to
solid food too abruptly, or return to a disease-producing diet. One must remember

that the more nearly normal his digestive system is, the more easily it is disturbed by wrong foods or wrong methods of eating.

Habits of wrong eating produce a condition of tolerance that is overcome by the fast and the milk diet—an excellent change toward permanent health. But one must also remember that the same factors which produced a disturbance in the first instance will, if returned to, produce the same condition, or some other abnormal change, and usually more quickly than at first.

When the time for stopping the milk diet arrives, it is almost invariably to be preferred that the milk be taken in the regular way until one or two o'clock in the afternoon; then nothing except water until five or six o'clock, when a meal consisting of vegetables, with or without vegetable soup, and whole wheat bread, and perhaps eggs may be eaten. The foods may be varied according to the desire of the patient. This plan is followed for at least from three days to one week, when the regular two or three meal plan is resumed, though there is no objection to following it for months. And, indeed, this may be done in many instances with much benefit, and I believe never with harm.

Some people have done extremely well by stopping the milk at noon, and for supper taking a very light meal consisting of a poached egg, and possibly a fruit salad. The next day they continue with the milk again as usual until noon, when once more they eat a "mixed meal"—slightly more substantial than the first one. And thus, by degrees, they gradually work back into an ordinary balanced diet once more.

From time to time a full day of milk drinking may be observed. Sunday is a good day for this. Or, if the combination milk and one meal plan is followed for a considerable time, an occasional day of solid food for all meals may be observed, but care must be taken that the variety and the nature of the food at these times be unproductive of disturbance.

I might mention also that it is many times of value to have one day of fasting occasionally, or to eat nothing but fruit, berries or melon.

Still later, after the "half-milk-one-meal" plan has been followed as long as desired, a quart of sweet milk, sumik, or buttermilk may be drunk for breakfast, with or without a piece of toast or a muffin, or a small amount of fruit. A light lunch and supper could make up the balance of the day's nutriment —probably a lunch of fruit, milk and nuts, and a vegetable dinner such as mentioned above.

Many times it is of advantage to continue using a considerable amount of milk, either to help build the blood more quickly, or to give the kidneys the benefit of a large amount of fluid, at the same time giving nourishment; or to give an easily digested diet in cases of stomach and intestinal weakness, etc., without requiring one to adhere rigidly to such a confining régime as milk exclusively.

The combination milk and one meal plan is of particular value in the following diseases and disorders: anemia, alcoholism, atony of the bowels and stomach, bladder diseases, colitis, constipation of an obstinate nature, diabetes, drug habits, dysentery and enteritis, emaciation or thinness, gastric ulcer or ulcers of the rectum or elsewhere in the digestive tract, goitre, heart disease, where the milk is especially recommended, hemorrhoids, influenza (after the fever has subsided), particularly if the energy returns slowly, malaria, neurasthenia, paralysis, ptomain poisoning, prolapsus of abdominal or pelvic organs, sexual, skin and splenic disorders, syphilis, tuberculosis, and vital depletion.

This régime will go far toward preventing a recurrence of the condition for which the milk treatment was taken in the first place, and will prove to be of genuine value as a health conservation practice. Many business men often plan to have a couple of quarts of milk delivered to their offices or their places of business, where they can take their milk in such quantities as will furnish them all the nutriment required until the next meal-time.

It might be well to mention here that, where possible, it will be good practice to let the milk stand several hours or over night in the ice-box and pour off the layer of cream which rises to the top—drinking the remainder as suggested elsewhere. And right here I might remark that milk which has been placed in the ice-box forms one-third more cream than milk which is kept at room temperature. This procedure will insure a more thorough removal of the fat content of the milk and enhance its digestibility. This should be remembered by those who, when on the full milk diet, should use skimmed milk, and the plan is especially recommended for hot weather, also for those inclined to obesity and those of the "bilious type."

Milk should not be frozen, however, and at least the chill should be removed before the milk is consumed.

Many find that on going back to solid food there is still a great desire for considerable milk. This may be taken freely, exclusively as a meal, or at carefully balanced meals at any time desired. But the great thirst most people experience after returning to solid food from the exclusive milk diet is because of a great reduction of imbibed liquid. This thirst should be satisfied, but not with milk if the diet is a well balanced solid food diet. Water only should be used in such instances, or fruit juice may be used, between meals or at meals that have been carefully balanced in consideration of the fruit juice to be taken. If milk is desired to satisfy this thirst care must be made to allow for it in quantity and combination of other foods.

AVOID AUTO-INTOXICATION AND CONSTIPATION

There is, obviously, no more definite reason for lowered vitality and lack of resistance than auto-intoxication from intestinal absorption. Auto-intoxication is present in more than two-thirds of all patients presenting themselves for relief from chronic conditions.

The condition is very readily diagnosed, the symptoms being headache, sleepiness, sleeplessness or disturbed sleep, dizziness, weariness, muscular weakness, nervous irritability, flatulence, foul stools, irregularities of appetite, furred tongue, bad breath, muddy complexion or skin eruption, offensive perspiration any one of these being present in any individual case. Also invariably there are strong evidences of the results of auto-intoxication appearing in the urine (which is usually highly colored) in the form of indican.

Indican appearing in the urine is absolute proof of putrefactive fermentation in the small intestine and that there is absorption of these toxic products into the general circulation, almost certainly with the development of symptoms of toxemia.

The predisposing cause of this trouble is constipation, resulting from over-eating, or inability of the digestive organs to take care of the food intake and to convert it into nourishing elements, or inability to expel their contained waste elements regularly and in requisite amounts.

The trouble most frequently starts in the

colon, extending gradually upward until the infective condition is more or less general. I can not too strongly emphasize the necessity of regular and adequate evacuation of the bowels in these and in all other conditions.

Whether this is accomplished by diet, by the enema, by exercise, by the liberal drinking of water, or by mineral oil, is more or less immaterial, but one should not rely regularly upon any such substances as intestinal lubricants or any such methods as the enema. The proper diet, proper exercise, and the drinking of water should be all that is necessary after correctly taking the milk diet. But it is very essential that the bowels be stimulated or, rather, adjusted to move regularly, and any method that is not harmful may be employed as occasion seems to demand.

In addition, however, I believe that it is possible to reduce the number of the intestinal germs by the use of lactic acid ferments, such as buttermilk, sumik, or sour milk, developed by the action of the Bulgarian bacillus, first advocated by Metchnikoff. This is the bacillus now known as the "bacillus of Massol." Hundreds of physicians and dieticians have attested the value of this bacillus in helping to create a food that will have a tendency to disinfect the colon.

There has been any amount of clinical evidence advanced as to the utility of this bacillus in preventing the propagation of harmful germs in the intestines. The use of naturally soured or "cultured" milks has been efficacious in thousands of instances in establishing or maintaining a normal eliminative action of the bowels and in preventing unnatural decomposition and fermentation in the digestive tract, thus allaying or preventing the development of toxemia.

I wish to emphasize the point, however, that any person who has a diet solely of sweet milk must necessarily develop numberless millions of the ordinary lactic acid bacilli, the immense number and the continuous action of which must have a pronounced effect upon the pathogenic or disease-producing bacteria in the intestinal tract. This proves to my mind that the sweet milk diet in itself will develop all the good effects ordinarily claimed for the use of lactic acid bacilli, no matter how expensive or difficult it may be to secure these, for it must be remembered that human nature is such that we are inclined to think of the more financially costly things as being the most beneficial or valuable.

Fresh fruits and fruit juices and fresh vegetables are excellent to keep the intestinal content of germs reduced—the fruit juices by their antiseptic action and the fresh vegetables by their tendency to keep the intestinal tract somewhat "scoured," thus preventing development of germs in large numbers.

THE RIGHT KIND OF FOOD

It would be well to bear in mind also that the building and maintaining of permanent good health is very largely a matter of correct diet. A well balanced diet with the proper amount of protein, carbohydrate and fats is most necessary. Protein, as you remember, embraces not only meat, fowl, fish, eggs and milk, but also peas, beans, and other vegetables rich in nitrogen, and cheese, nuts, and whole wheat.

Once a day should be often enough to use meat. Every second day or twice a week would be better for most people. Then the meat should either be boiled, broiled or baked —never fried. Veal and pork should be avoided as much as possible, although if a pork chop or pork tenderloin is steamed for an hour or so, with tomato sauce or some similar appetizing dressing, it is usually quite tender and extremely digestible and may be used occasionally.

Mackerel, blue-fish and eels should be avoided by many people, as they contain too much fat and are likely to prove indigestible.

Recalling that milk has considerable protein, you will appreciate the fact that milk should not be used with meats or other protein.

I can not too strongly condemn all demineralized foods, such as white bread and white crackers, and other white flour products. In their place should be used whole wheat bread, graham and whole wheat crackers, and other whole wheat products. Also scoured oat-meal, polished rice and tapioca, cornstarch and corn flakes should be taboo, and, in their stead, unscoured whole oatmeal, brown rice, whole corn-meal mush, and other foods containing the calcium, magnesium, sodium, iron, potassium, silica, and other vital mineral salts of the entire grain should be used.

While these cereals and cereal products are to a considerable extent protein foods, they are also carbohydrate and fat foods, as they contain the various primary food elements in well balanced form when the entire grain is used. Other wholesome carbohydrate foods are sweet fruits, honey, sweet and white potatoes (which are always preferably baked) and young corn, peas and beans.

The list of satisfactory fats is very small. Cream and butter head the list in digestibility and value. Then there are peanut butter and oil, and olive oil. Animal fats should be used sparingly unless prolonged experience has proven them to be beneficial in your case.

Fruit, especially oranges and grapefruit, should be eaten every day, not only for the mineral salts they contain, but also for the stimulating effect these fruits have upon the liver and organs of excretion. In addition to these, all other fruits, berries and melon should be used in season—taking care that combinations are correct.

Many times it is not necessary or possible to continue the use of large quantities of milk, in which cases plenty of water should be taken daily to supply the body with sufficient solvent liquid. This water should rarely be distilled, but should, on the contrary, practically always be natural, unaltered water, if the source of the water and the water itself are uncontaminated.

CARE NECESSARY IN GOITRE CASES

Particular care should be exercised by goitre patients in returning to a general diet once more. For goitre largely depends for its existence upon toxic irritation of the thyroid gland. The chief source of this irritation is in the abnormal fermentation in the intestinal canal and in the absorption into the blood stream of the poisons there generated.

So, to avoid any possible recurrence of the condition, I would advise a light diet, with very little meat and a "part time" régime of milk, or an exclusive milk diet at least once or twice a year until all signs of the enlargement of the thyroid and of its toxic effects have disappeared.

This will not only prevent the goitrous condition from returning, but it will materially help the general health and assist greatly in building it up.

The combination milk diet and vegetable meal plan is especially to be recommended in these cases, and the plan may be continued indefinitely.

Many times conditions are such that it is not possible to continue the full milk diet longer than to receive a good start toward health. The proper régime adopted at the finish of the milk diet will further the improvement. This, of course, holds true in any abnormal condition.

WEIGHT GAINED FROM THE MILK DIET

Many women are needlessly worried when taking the milk treatment, fearing that the increase in flesh produced thereby may prove permanent. I can assure these women that the increase in the waist measurement, in the hips, or in the size of the bust is only transient, if abnormal, and will rapidly disappear after the milk diet has been discontinued for a week or two and after they become more active again.

It is only in cases where the additional weight is necessary to bring about normality that it is permanent, and frequently here only if a weight-retaining régime is adopted and adhered to.

No condition of obesity has ever been developed while taking the milk diet. Milk does not create flabby fat. It is a corrective diet for tissues below par, and it aids these tissues and the entire body to approach normality. This means that an improvement is established in the "selective action" of the cells, by which action they are enabled to discard elements not necessary for natural growth, repair and bodily functions. Worthless, unsightly, cumbersome or burdensome fat is therefore never developed or deposited from a milk diet.

The usual rule is that where the flesh is built up solidly this flesh is healthy, normal tissue, and it is natural that it should remain. Where it is somewhat in excess of the physiological requirements it will be used up in a very short time by active exercise or it will disappear by chemical alteration and absorption.

On the contrary, the healthy stimulation from, and the natural tonic effect of the milk diet persists sometimes for many months. For something of definite health value has been built into every individual cell in the body to become part of its make-up, and contributes its quota in raising the entire body to a better and more perfect functioning power.

In order that the greatest future value as well as the immediate benefit of the milk diet may be obtained. it is therefore essential that the most rational régime be selected and followed. Your system will have become more attuned to Nature by the remedial milk diet régime, and it can be kept in this high or higher degree of efficiency by allowing the reawakened or more active vital force to manifest itself, unembarrassed and unobstructed by a wilful, careless or thoughtless opposition.

CHAPTER VI

How to Keep the Health You Have Gained

WHAT HAS ALREADY BEEN ACCOMPLISHED IN YOUR CASE. — AVOID REPEATING HARMFUL HABITS. — MAKE "MODERATION" YOUR WATCHWORD.—RELAXATION AND DEEP BREATHING.—A WHOLESOME SEX LIFE NECESSARY.—PLENTY OF SLEEP.— SLEEP ALONE IF POSSIBLE. — CONTINUE WITH THE BATHS.—BATHING DURING MENSTRUATION.— WARM BUT LOOSE AND POROUS CLOTHING BEST. —DO NOT CRAMP THE BODY OR FEET.—DON'T READ TOO MUCH.—EXERCISE AND RECREATION.— DRINK PLENTY OF WATER.—MILK USEFUL TO PRESERVE AS WELL AS TO RESTORE HEALTH.—MILK FOODS. — WATCH YOUR WEIGHT. — THE YEARLY PHYSICAL INVENTORY AND EXAMINATION.—FINAL SUGGESTIONS.—SUMMARY OF MILK DIET.

ALMOST invariably those who have taken the milk cure properly will find themselves in better health than they may ever have enjoyed before. The body cells are "clean." They are relatively free from organic toxins.

The elimination is better. The organs of

digestion and assimilation function in a more natural way. The blood is enriched and purified, as a consequence of which oxidation proceeds more normally.

The nerves and the brain cells are nourished. There is usually a capacity for an immensely increased amount of both mental and physical work. There is also a distinct increase in sexual tone, with the additional increase in general energy resulting therefrom.

Needless to say, if the healthful gain made on the milk diet is to have any permanent beneficial effect, "moderation" must be the watchword in everything.

The greatest care must be observed so that the body, the mind, or any special organs shall not become fatigued in their functions. Periods of rest should be taken. Long stretches of mental concentration should be avoided. The mind should be diverted every once in a while—when it is found to be more or less of an effort to concentrate on the subject under consideration or on the work of the moment.

If it is only to get up from the desk and go over to the window and look out for a minute or two, you should make an attempt to do this.

At night a couple of hours spent at a concert, a lecture, seeing a good "show" or moving picture, or an hour or two spent with an interesting book or magazine, will go far to divert the mind and give it that recreation and rest so essential to proper functioning.

I hardly need again caution against over-indulgence in sexual intercourse, which so often follows the invigorating effect of a full "tonic" diet. Common sense must be the guide in these matters, remembering always that energy which is not dissipated is a very distinct asset to the sum total of well-being.

PLENTY OF SLEEP

Sleep is, next to proper food, the greatest reconstructive force we have. For, I may here again emphasize, it is only during sleep that the final processes of assimilation are completed.

It is during these hours that the assimilated pabulum from food digestion is converted into active cells and living vital tissues.

Therefore get plenty of sleep. At least eight hours' sleep a night is necessary for complete rehabilitation of wasted energy and the reconstruction and rebuilding of broken down tissue for the majority of people.

If you are inclined to be delicate and nervous, even ten hours is none too much. Remember it is quite impossible to get *too much sleep*. For when the body and the mind are thoroughly rested, you'll wake up, rested and refreshed. You couldn't sleep any more even if you wanted to.

Sleep always in a well ventilated room, and if it is at all possible, in a separate bed. For the restlessness of one sleeper is quite likely to affect the other, and the more profound the sleep and the least disturbed it is, the quicker the recuperation and the more good you'll get out of it.

Another thing, there is a certain loss of magnetism sustained by certain susceptible individuals, particularly children and young people, who are obliged to sleep with the aged or with people much older than themselves or those with waning bodily energies.

In fact, it used to be a custom in France many years ago for decrepit noblemen or wealthy men and women to hire a young and vigorous individual—usually of the opposite sex—to sleep with them. The younger person invariably lost vitality from this contact. Finally, however, this strange sale of vitality was forbidden by law.

And now the sleeping relation is only practiced because of ignorance of its deleterious consequences or because stress of economic conditions enforces it.

CONTINUE THE BATHS

I can not too strongly emphasize the valuable effects of the daily warm bath as a means of keeping the pores open and helping to rid the body of poisons that might otherwise accumulate there, or else force extra work of elimination upon the kidneys, lungs, and bowels.

177

The cleansing bath should be followed, if possible, with a cold shower or sponge bath, provided the shock of the cold water is not too great. Or else the warm water can be run out of the tub while the cold water is being run in. Splash around meanwhile, until just a comfortable degree of coolness is experienced, or start with comfortable coolness and daily lower the temperature slightly until cold baths can be taken with pleasure.

The bath should invariably be followed by a brisk rub with a coarse towel. This will stimulate the better activity of the surface capillaries, bring the blood tingling to the surface of the body, and stir up a wholesome activity in the pores of the skin.

Many women abstain from the general, or tub bath during the menstrual period, believing that bathing at this time tends to suppress the menstrual flow. This may be the case with certain individuals, but the great majority of women can enjoy comfort and the delightful feeling of cleanliness that follows a warm bath without any apprehension of suppressing their period.

This, of course, does not apply to cold baths or to sea bathing, to excessively hot baths, or to any exposure which might prove a distinct shock to the system. However, if reasonable care be observed, there is no reason why women should deprive themselves of the gratification of a warm bath a day or so after the height of the flow has subsided.

THE CLOTHING

No one, unless very anemic, is justified in swathing himself or herself in heavy clothing practically impervious to the passage of air.

Even in the coldest weather decently light clothing should be worn, together with open-mesh underwear that will permit the entrance of fresh air to the skin cells and facilitate the liberation of the noxious gases thrown off by the skin, the retention of which will poison just as surely as would the swallowing of the same quantity of poisons.

With reasonably light clothes the circulation of the skin is improved, the oxidation processes of the body will be assisted, a more equable degree of heat will be maintained, and as a consequence more food will be conserved and utilized, because the digestive and assimilative processes will be greatly improved.

Too many people are prone to jump into heavier undergarments at the slightest suspicion of cold. Having done so, they render themselves more vulnerable to attacks of cold, influenza, rheumatism and other troubles, because the effect of the heavy garments is to create an undue amount of heat, especially during the hours they spend in their homes, offices, or places of business, if engaged in inside work. And where the body is supplied heat without effort it will not manufacture its own heat—its circulation will not be normally vigorous, and therefore elimination will be defective and deficient.

Therefore it is always wise to wear such weight garments as shall keep the skin in a state of normal activity, trusting to nourishing food, deep breathing and vigorous exercise to give you all the oxidation necessary to keep you comfortable and warm even in the coldest weather.

The same thing is true of extremely heavy shoes, or shoes that are too tight to permit the feet to "breathe" and the blood to flow through them. In the winter-time a cramped foot is usually a cold foot.

A foot encased in a shoe long enough and wide enough to permit the one-half inch deviation in length and the three-fourths of an inch increase in breadth that follows putting the weight of the body on the foot is the foot that will remain warm, no matter what reasonable degree of exposure it be subject to.

DON'T READ TOO MUCH

While I heartily approve of reading for diversion, I can not too strongly condemn "exhaustive reading." By this I mean the kind of reading done by certain individuals who get hold of a book and who are not content to put it away until they have finished it, or else until they are so tired and sleepy that they can no longer hold their eyes open.

This sort of reading is worse than none

at all. Remember that the function of seeing, translating the characters or letters into
ideas, and the conveying of these ideas to the
brain uses up one-third of the total expended
energy of the brain.

Multiply this by the continued hours of
reading, many of which perhaps should be
spent in sleeping, and you will form some
idea of the amount of energy that can be
dissipated needlessly in what should be a
profitable recreation.

The same thing is true of sewing or knitting, especially sewing and knitting on fine
work that entails considerable eye-strain.

There are many women who are not content to sit quiet for five minutes unless their
needles are flying back and forth or unless
they can feel they are accomplishing some
constructive task.

As a matter of fact, all the hemstitching
and beautiful embroidery you or any other
woman can do in a year is not worth the
physical and mental expense it entails.

Suppose you do have to buy machine-
hemmed tablecloths, napkins and dresser

scarfs. What of it? They may not look quite as well as the hand-worked variety, but, weighed against the value of the amount of useful energy you will save, they'll look mighty well, especially when you find yourself with so much more time and energy on your hands that can be diverted to the comfort or companionship of your husband or the children.

EXERCISE AND RECREATION

One of the foremost essentials of right living is exercise. The object of exercise is to improve the circulation and the general nutrition by developing better breathing power and better general nutrition.

Readers of PHYSICAL CULTURE Magazine will need no special instructions in respect to the value of exercise in maintaining better physical functioning. As every reader of PHYSICAL CULTURE knows, every muscle, in contracting, uses up a definite amount of food carried to it in the blood. The arteries and blood vessels carrying this blood become dilated and enlarged, in order to carry the necessary food elements and oxygen to the parts.

Perhaps the best, cheapest, and most available of all forms of exercise is walking. Walking exercises most of the muscles of the body, produces deeper respiration, and consequently better oxidation, and helps the peristaltic action of the muscles of the stomach and bowels. Food is better digested, and the food debris is more effectively got rid of. The blood circulates more freely, and every cell and gland in the body is enriched by an additional supply of the nutrient substances brought in contact with it.

In the Summer and Fall, swimming, rowing, and tennis offer pleasurable opportunities for active physical recreation. Tennis is valuable to develop litheness, agility, elasticity, and as a general conditioning exercise. Swimming and rowing are especially good for those physically fit to indulge in them, for these exercises bring into active play the abdominal and back muscles and various groups of muscles that are not greatly influenced by walking and many other exercises.

Golf, of course, also furnishes this stimulus to the abdominal and back muscles, but not every one can afford the time or the expense to devote to golf two or three afternoons a week. Horseback riding, notwithstanding its admitted value, is equally out of the question because of its generally prohibitive expense to most city dwellers.

EXERCISE IN WINTER

There is probably no single season of the year that is best for health and for recovering health. Each season has its advantages. Perhaps there is no better time for building rich red blood and for increasing the circulation to its greatest efficiency than the Winter. For this season offers some of the most wholesome of exercises and activity, and this, with the lowered temperature and apparently fresher air, which lend energy to the nervous system, makes exercise a pleasure.

Skating, which may be considered in effect midway between walking and running, can be secured in a valuable form only in the Winter. Indoor skating can be secured in some places out of season, but at such times it is possible to indulge in those equally enjoyable and more valuable outdoor sports of the particular season.

Skiing, snow-shoeing, ice-boat sailing, and treading through the snow, or even over clear roads in the Winter-time, are positive health producers. If one can relax from his dignity and has the opportunity, tobogganing is also excellent—mainly because of the climb to the top of the hill again, and also because of the spirit of youthfulness in which this sport is indulged in.

The exercises just given are more on the order of sports, but are among the most wholesome of exercises because taken under the most favorable conditions of air, sunshine and association. But for reasons of circumstances at this time, business, location, etc., some people can not take advantage of these sports.

There are innumerable forms of exercise that can be taken alone and in the privacy of one's home or bedroom. If one has a phonograph or radio outfit, he can exercise regularly, and with pleasure and benefit, to the rhythmic swing of music. But even these are not necessary.

One may have dumb-bells, Indian clubs, chest or wall machine, bar-bells, etc., for regular exercise of value. But some of the most beneficial of all exercises may be taken without apparatus of any kind, though if one wishes he may use books or pieces of furniture for his "gymnasium apparatus."

Because relaxation can be secured where or when desired, reclining exercises on the bed or floor are particularly helpful in many cases, and valuable in all.

Stretching and breathing exercises should be taken at least once a day by everyone. The morning is the best time for these, and they may be taken before arising from bed, but the covers should be thrown down before these are taken.

Resistive exercises and the muscle tensing exercises can be made as slight or as vigorous as desired; in fact, they can be made as strenuous as exercises with the bar-bell. If relaxation is thorough and efficient after such exercises, they are among the best for all round development and "conditioning."

Thus it will be seen that if one is anxious enough for health he will have no such excuse as not being equipped for exercise. The matter of exercise is one that each individual must solve for himself—based on his opportunities, economic condition, physical ability, and preferences. I can only emphasize that adequate provision must be made for it, if the best effects on health are to be obtained and maintained.

DRINK PLENTY OF WATER

I would reiterate, also, the necessity of drinking from six to ten glasses of pure cool (not iced) water every day, preferably between meals, on a more or less empty stomach. The best time to drink water is on rising in the morning, between meals, before meals, with possibly one glass at each meal.

If the drinking of much fluid in the evening tends to break sleep by getting one up to urinate it would be well to avoid drinking water after supper at night, so as to give the kidneys and bladder as little to do as possible during the night, though a definite thirst should be satisfied regardless of the time of day or night.

In this matter, also, good judgment will indicate the proper course and ultimately indicate the plan of action best calculated to give the most satisfying results.

CONTINUE TO DRINK MILK

I would also urge that every man, woman and child, where it is at all possible, drink at least a quart of milk each and every day.

This may be taken as a beverage, or as buttermilk or clabbered or fermented milk, or taken in oyster stews, milk toast, milk foods—such as custard and milk soups—or on cereals, or any way so long as the requisite amount of milk be taken each day. But attempt to get some raw milk, even though prepared milk foods and cooked milks are used.

Few people realize what delicious dishes can be made from the rennet junket tablets, sold at most drug and grocery stores, for making junket desserts. These desserts are much more wholesome, digestible and nutritious than pies, pudding and other commonly used desserts. Therefore it is a great pity that they are not more generally employed as valuable food products.

And remember that one chief reason for taking milk persistently is the fact that it is rich in those vitally essential food products—vitamines.

In discussing this subject, Prof. M. J. Rosenau, of the Harvard Medical School, says:

"Milk is rich in all of the known vitamines. We would rather expect this to be the case, for the mammalian suckling must depend upon milk as its sole source of food supply for a fairly long period of time. Milk, in fact, is the only single article of food that fairly represents a complete diet. Milk is unexcelled for growing children; it has no equal for the promotion of growth and nutrition. Furthermore, cow's milk is rich in calcium in a readily available form—children need five times as much calcium per kilo (about 2.2 pounds) of body weight as adults. In order to supply this important salt to growing bones and developing teeth, as well as to furnishing vitamines for the utilization of food, a child should drink a quart of milk a day. It will not then suffer from a deficiency disease. In this sense, milk is well called a protective food."

WATCH YOUR WEIGHT

One of the surest general indexes in determining health, or the state of nutrition upon which health depends, is the maintenance of normal weight.

First and foremost it is necessary to be sure that you are not materially under weight or over weight for your height.

Tables of weight in relation to height and age are given in many books and circulars; also they will be found on penny scales. It must be remembered, however, that these weights are for the *average* individual, and they are also usually *above the strictly normal* for individual heights, because the average individual is above normal in weight.

Those who are naturally and normally slender, or of the "race-horse type," and those who are heavily built, or of the "draft-horse type," are all taken into consideration in the making of these tables. It is utterly wrong for one normally above or below the average given to attempt to reach down to or up to the weight given. The older the individual, the farther below the weights given in these tables should he go, for greatest health and safety.

It might be stated that up to thirty it is frequently better if one can add weight to, or somewhat above the average for that age. The increased weight if constituted of normal tissue will be apt to protect the individual from such conditions as anemia, tuberculosis, and general depletion due to the expenditure of a great amount of energy during youth.

Usually, from twenty-eight to thirty five or forty, one is inclined to put on excessive weight, or weight above the average. This is due frequently to a continuation of the same dietetic habits as during greater physical activity, or a great reduction of that physical activity, or both. A man's "dignity" frequently prevents him at this age from being natural and giving vent to his surplus energies in wholesome, care-free activity of a physical nature. Not having an escape in this manner, the excessive food and energy are stored up in an unnecessary increase in flesh.

It is frequently in the decade from thirty to forty that many future illnesses have their beginning. One should endeavor during this time to hold his weight in check if it is inclined to rise above the average, or what can be determined to be normal for him.

After forty, or at least fifty, it is better by far that the weight be allowed to go gradually below the average than above. It is well, of course, if the average or normal weight can be maintained, but it should not be allowed to go above the normal, or at most not more than a very few pounds.

It is frequently those "who are the picture of health" who are slowly developing a thick, viscid blood, hardened arteries, and a high blood pressure, also kidney trouble, liver trouble, diabetes, or some other disorder, due primarily to an excess of nourishment and a deficiency of solvent fluids and foods and of wholesome corrective physical activity.

THE YEARLY EXAMINATION

Every year one should take a physical inventory to determine the health and normal functioning of every organ, gland, and structure of the body. However, unless one has made a study of anatomy and physiology he is not apt to interpret properly his findings. For this reason it is a good plan to have a thorough physical examination yearly. If possible, this examination should be made by one who has specialized in health preservation rather than merely the treatment of diseases and disorders after they have become established. In rural communities this will be difficult, perhaps, but in all cities and most towns of considerable size will be found those who can give a satisfactory examination and an interpretation of conditions found.

If it is not desired or not possible for any reason to have a complete physical examination yearly, at least a urinalysis and a blood pressure examination should be made. If any abnormal conditions are found, steps should be instituted at once toward their correction, rather than delay for some "better time" or in the hope that they will right themselves.

FINAL SUGGESTIONS

There is no secret in preserving health and long life. It is merely required that we live according to natural laws, that we prevent— by proper diet, exercise, baths, fresh air, and sleep—the formation of those poisons within the body that handicap, cripple, and kill. This should be self-evident.

Tobacco, alcohol, and drugs of all kinds should be taboo. Excessive indulgence in candy, ice cream and sweets, and over-eating of any sort of food must be rigidly guarded against.

The proper frame of mind must be cultivated. It is not necessary to become a fanatic. The highest possible degree of cheerfulness, courage and confidence must be maintained. Let the mind and the physiological processes that the mind governs work constructively. Let them build up, not tear down—speaking in the broad health sense.

So convinced am I of the disease-correcting and health-maintaining power of the fast and milk diet that I urge any one who has an abnormal functional or organic condition, especially in the beginning or in the incipient stage, to adopt this means of re-establishing normality.

If these two factors were employed regularly as a health-conservation measure, drug practice would be reduced ninety per cent.

Every year or two, merely for the sake of maintaining health, it would be a good plan to take a short fast and a short course of the milk diet, in order to maintain the highest degree of health and efficiency possible for the remainder of the year.

And remember that, in nine hundred and ninety-nine cases out of a thousand, you have it in your own power, merely by exercising discrimination, judgment, and restraint, to live out your allotted span of years in health and in the comfort, happiness, and economic stability that health brings. And more than this no reasonable person can demand.

A SUMMARY OF THE MILK DIET

1. *A proper preparatory treatment* is necessary for most satisfactory results. Fruit juice only, an absolute fast, or a combination of these two prepares the digestive and assimilative organs for the new diet.

2. *Use the purest milk obtainable,* and from Holstein, or at least some other breed of cows than Jersey or Guernsey if possible. The flavor is improved by aerating it—by pouring from pitcher to pitcher, or shaking it in some other way.

3. *Unpasteurized milk* is preferable, though pasteurized milk may be used when necessary.

4. *The proper method of taking the milk* is the method used by the nursing baby in sucking its milk from the bottle. This is done by placing the edge of the lips close to the rim of the glass and making the opening between the lips so small that considerable suction will be required to draw the milk into

the mouth. This process not only mixes the saliva with the milk but very greatly improves the flavor.

5. *In regard to the quantity,* the average case may use to best advantage a quart of milk to each twenty-five to thirty-five pounds of body weight. Another guide is one quart of milk for each foot in height, for men, and three or four ounces less for women. Roughly, five quarts daily for women of average size and six quarts daily for men of average size will be approximately correct.

6. *Constipation* is not infrequently produced at the beginning of the milk diet. Do not discontinue the milk, but take a small enema of about half a pint of warm or cool water each morning or, if necessary, each morning and evening.

7. *Diarrhea* also is sometimes induced by the milk diet. This is because of abnormal body conditions and is not due to the milk directly. It may be remedied by simply lessening the quantity of milk. Reducing the cream or diluting the milk will sometimes be all that is necessary. In some cases a high,

warm, full enema is valuable. In others the difficulty does not respond satisfactorily to any of the above methods. In these it may be advisable to use a few dates a day—as many as two to four with each glass of milk. In other obstinate cases it will be necessary to take the milk until noon, and an ordinary meal in the evening, or, take a breakfast, and then take milk all afternoon, beginning at twelve or one.

8. *Nausea* is not infrequently caused by the milk. This can be remedied by taking acid fruits or their juices, preferably lemon, or grape-fruit or orange, either just before or just after the milk, or at any time that nausea is experienced. Removal of some of the cream or diluting the milk may help, also.

9. *A sense of fullness* in the abdominal region is nearly always produced by the milk diet. This need occasion no alarm. It is only natural that a large quantity of nourishing liquid should produce a fullness and stretching of the digestive tract and abdominal tissues. It will usually subside before

the completion of the diet, and always on the return to the regular diet.

10. *A coated tongue, unpleasant taste* in the mouth, and *unpleasant breath,* are often noticeable when first beginning the diet, especially on rising in the morning. The symptoms should cause no worry, as they usually disappear in a short time. In some cases the tongue is coated during the entire milk diet period, without interfering in the least with the benefits of the diet.

11. *A milk diet means a milk diet*—nothing else. Don't add other foods promiscuously. The only exceptions are in cases of some disagreement of the milk, due to an abnormal condition of the digestive channel, when fruits or fruit juices may be taken as fully explained. Combinations of milk and other foods, usually fruits, may be valuable in many cases, but do not consider this the *milk diet.*

12. *Water* is rarely required when on the milk diet, except the first thing in the morning. But if at any time of the day or night there is a genuine thirst for water only,

there will be no harm whatever in taking any amount desired.

13. *The warm, neutral bath,* 98 to 99 degrees Fahrenheit, can usually be taken with advantage while on this diet. Start the water at 95 degrees and gradually increase it to that desired, up to 99 degrees. Remain in the water, fully relaxed, from half an hour to an hour.

14. *Exercise* is sometimes to be rigidly avoided. If you are taking a fairly large quantity of milk it is sometimes desirable to be lazy—to have little or no physical activity. Many cases, however, do better while exercising. The most satisfactory time is the first thing in the morning, before taking any milk.

15. *The length of time required* to secure desired results on the milk diet varies greatly —from three to four weeks to as many months—or even as many years in a few serious organic diseases. The average is probably five to six weeks. Much depends upon inherent vitality, age, nature, extent and duration of the disorder, previous treat-

ment, previous surgical interference, preparation for and application of the treatment, etc. Do not be discouraged if marked improvement is not noticed within a few days. Adhere to the treatment, modifying it only when necessary, and results will come if they can be secured at all.

16. *Old symptoms,* long ago suppressed and forgotten, may return after a few weeks or even after a few days of the milk. These are due to the healing nature of the diet, which flushes the tissues, carries out diseased cells and waste, brings repair nourishment to the affected parts, and increases the circulation and nerve action to and through the region formerly diseased. These symptoms should not worry you—they pass off as the structures and functions are returned to more nearly normal.

17. *Changing from a milk diet* to the regular diet requires caution, regardless of the improvement made on the diet. The digestive and all other functions are greatly improved and, because more nearly normal than before, they are more easily and quickly af-

fected by any abnormal or unnatural influence. The benefits derived from the milk diet régime may be retained and even added to by using care in selecting a wholesome diet and mode of living generally.

[THE END]

CPSIA information can be obtained at www.ICGtesting.com
Printed in the USA
LVOW07s1041151114

413869LV00001B/34/P